ADVANCE PRAISE
THE RICHEST KIDS I...

"Mark has hit on the two keys to our future success—kids and entre-preneurialism. This book eliminates excuses and provides inspirational anecdotes to which we all should aspire. If these kids can do it, so can you and me. I am now doubling the size of my goals! Bravo Mark!"

—**Darren Hardy,** Publisher, *Success* Magazine

"Don't worry; this is not just 'another' teen manual! This book is a powerful collection of creative ideas and personal stories that makes the process of becoming a successful leader fun while offering the tools to become a profitable business owner. Opportunities are all around you and the first one is the book the book you now hold in your hands. The content is practical and the impact is powerful. I've personally learned many invaluable lessons from Mark and now he is sharing them with you. Every young person who wants an extraordinary life should read this book!"

—**Kent Healy**, author of *"Cool Stuff" They Should Teach in School* and *The Success Principles for Teens*

"Mark Victor Hansen does it again—*The Richest Kids in America* will get you moving in the direction of your dreams, fast!"

—**Keith Ferrazzi**, author of *Never Eat Alone* and *Who's Got Your Back*

"Having interviewed some 26,000 children over the last 25 years to prove that *Kids Say the Darndest Things*, I now discover a new book by my friend Mark Victor Hansen called *The Richest Kids in America* and I would certainly recommend it for anyone who is interested in the way children think and what they can do when it comes to making money. Having started my own first independent business selling lemons in the back of the packing plant which had been rejected, at the age of 11, I have keen regard for these marvelous kids who have made it at an early age. It took me another 25 years to be in their class. Enjoy this fascinating glimpse into the minds and activity of some of our future multimillionaires."

—**Art Linkletter**, host and bestselling author of *Kids Say the Darndest Things*

ADVANCE PRAISE FOR
THE RICHEST KIDS IN AMERICA

"Mark Victor Hansen has once again delivered a message that can and will transform lives, open minds, touch hearts and inspire people to reach their highest potential. *The Richest Kids in America* will make a huge and critical contribution to all who read it. Bravo! to Mark for continuing to break ground and help us all to break through any barriers to being the best we can be."

—**Lynne Twist,** bestselling author of *The Soul of Money*

"Wow! Don't I wish this book had been available when I was a kid. It would have saved me tens of thousands of dollars and an enormous amount of time. This should be required reading in all public schools."

—**Robert G. Allen,** bestselling author of *Nothing Down, Creating Wealth, Multiple Streams of Income, Multiple Streams of Internet Income* and co-author of *The One Minute Millionaire*

Please Share With Us

We would love to hear your reaction to the stories in this book. Please let us know what your favorite stories were and how they affected you.

We also invite you to send us stories you would like to see published in future editions of the ***Richest Kids*** book series. You can either send us stories of your experience or the stories of other young entrepreneurs that you have met or interviewed.

Please send stories to:

Mark Victor Hansen
P.O. Box 7665
Newport Beach, California 92627
Fax: 1-949-722-6912
e-mail: stories@markvictorhansen.com

We hope you enjoy reading this book as much as we enjoyed creating, writing, and editing it for you.

THE RICHEST KIDS IN AMERICA

how they earn it
how they spend it
how you can too

MARK VICTOR HANSEN

HANSEN HOUSE

HansenHousePublishing.com

The Richest Kids in America
How They Earn It, How They Spend It, How You Can Too

ISBN: 978-0-9819709-0-5

Inspiration / Self-Help / Business

1st edition, July 2009

Printed in the United States of America

HANSEN HOUSE

HansenHousePublishing.com

P O Box 7665
Newport Beach, CA 92658

Cover design, book layout and typography:
Chaz DeSimone
chazdesimone.com

*To all young Entrepreneurs,
their Parents, Teachers
and Mentors*

CONTENTS

DREAM BIG 1

SECTION 1
Creating Money with Your...

1 *Curiosity to Creativity to Cash* 9

2 *Purposeful Passion* 21

3 *The Spirit of Learning, Earning and Returning* 31

Superstar at a Glance: **CAMERON JOHNSON** 43

SECTION 2
Making it Work

4 *Turn Problems into Profits* 61

5 *Grow Rich in Your Niche* 75

6 *Dream Teamers* 85

Superstar at a Glance: **AKIANE KRAMIRAK** 93

SECTION 3
Building a Brand to Command

7 *The Biz of Biz-ness* 107

8 *Infinite Time* 115

9 *Giving to Make a Living* 123

LIVE BIG 131

BONUS SECTION
Business Strategies from Allyson Ames 135

Resources to Riches 143

Acknowledgments 149

About the Author 151

DREAM
BIG

Dreaming fuels us. It invigorates us. It moves us to take chances and step outside of our comfort zone. It is in our control. We can either dream small or dream big. We set our own limits just as we create our own expectations. So who says that a dream has to be something you long for in the future?

Why does a dream have to be far away, just out of reach? What would happen if you made your dream come true right now, today? How would your life be different if you decided to move without hesitation towards the one thing, that when you close your eyes and think about it, makes you feel truly alive?

I am here to tell you to open your eyes and embrace your dream this very moment. There is no reason to wait until you are older, until you have more education, until your bank account is larger. Open your mind to expand your thinking and seize every opportunity that presents itself to you. Open your heart to receive all of the greatness that comes with living your dream, your purpose, and sharing it with others.

My name is Mark Victor Hansen and I have been fortunate to be living my dream, my purpose, of impacting people's lives permanently and profitably, for over 30 years. My speaking, writing and entre-preneurship is the joy of my soul. I am proof that you can be, do and have all that you desire. It is as simple as tuning in to your inner guidance system and turning up the volume so you can take in every bit that it is telling you. It may be difficult to hear your own voice at first, considering there are so many distractions in this world that can take us away from our purpose. But over time, you will realize that your inner voice, your inner wisdom, is the one that is pushing you, supporting you and inspiring you. The more you acknowledge it, the clearer and louder it will become.

And do you know the most exciting part? It is your choice!

So many of your decisions each day—what to wear, what to eat, who to talk to, what to watch on television, where to put your focus—are dependent on whether or not you listen to your inner voice. How you view the world around you is determined by that one choice. It has more power than you may have ever imagined and can bring about hope that otherwise was not present before.

I am a true believer that hope gives options and options change lives and brighten your future. The young entrepreneurs that you will meet throughout the pages of this book are the ultimate examples of this philosophy, not only because they are living their dream life today, but because they are generous enough to share their story with you.

At the highest level of thinking, I believe these tremendous young people can motivate all of us to innovate and create businesses that will get the world's economy rocking again. Their stories captivated me and stirred me to new action and better results. I know that you will be as wowed as I am by their purpose, passion, processes, payoffs, contribution and make-it-happen determination.

When I first started learning about these extraordinary young entrepreneurs, I could not help but notice the similarities between them. Each of them was using principles and techniques that are available to all of us, yet only utilized by what seems like a select few. I was compelled to find out what made them different. How were they introduced to these concepts? What made them take the initiative to implement them into their lives? Where did they get their support and their encouragement? How did they handle obstacles and setbacks?

Questions are powerful tools, and by asking the right ones, patterns started to emerge. As I personally interviewed each of them, I began to see there were key distinctions that they all had in common and that made them so successful. It is my pleasure to share these points with you, so that you can come to realize your own greatness.

In my bestselling book, *The One Minute Millionaire: The Enlightened Way to Wealth*, co-authored with Robert G. Allen, I said there are a million ways to make a million dollars and there is one right, original and perfect way for you. That has become increasingly true and I want you to create something unique, innovative, omni-beneficial and profitable just like the entrepreneurs in this book.

I want to be able to tell YOUR story in future editions of this book series. It is my sincere hope that when you go out and conquer the world, you will visit me at MarkVictorHansen.com and let me know all that you have done.

You can submit your own story to stories@MarkVictorHansen.com

So are you ready? Let the journey begin! We are about to discover the Richest Kids in America, how they got that way and how you can do it too!

CREATING MONEY WITH YOUR...

I AM CREATIVE
I am creative...

I am creative.

I am allowing my creativity to flow through me.

It is exciting and delighting.

I enjoy experiencing and expressing my creative genius.

I have full permission to let it gush forth from my inner awareness.

The more I use my creativity, amazingly, the more I have.

I am enthusiastically turned on being creative.

I love the purposefulness, process and especially the payoffs of my creativity.

My creativity has creativity. My mind is out picturing exactly what my world needs, wants, desires and will cheerfully pay for now.

My mind is tapped in, turned on and blissfully turns out great and profitable ideas, services and products.

I am constantly being asked to use my creativity to come up with new solutions and ideas that will solve pressing problems. It is enjoyable to so positively use my wonderful imagination.

My creative imagination was a free gift from God, I value it as truly priceless and want to use it for the highest and best good always.

The positive response I get for my creativity is wondrous, magnificent and soul-satisfying.

My productivity produces profits, bank accounts, happy customers, paid employees, grateful vendors and suppliers and puts me in a state of absolute joy.

I remember that the world's greatest inventor, Thomas Alva Edison, said of creativity, "If we did all the things we are capable of doing, we would literally astonish ourselves."

I am here to astonish myself and everyone else with my ever-flowing and overflowing creativity.

CHAPTER 1

CURIOSITY TO CREATIVITY TO CASH

For many of us, the most successful "kids" we can think of are those that are famous in pop culture. This makes sense because they are the ones that are in front of us, on television, in the movies, on the radio and featured on the covers of magazines. These famous kids are talented, driven and highly publicized. We know their stories and follow their every move as they live in the spotlight.

If you excel in the field of entertainment, there is a great deal of recognition that comes with it. Justin Timberlake, Christina Aguilera and Hillary Duff grew up personally and professionally before our eyes. And those are just a few in the last decade alone.

And while these teen sensations deserve our praise and our interest, I believe there is another group of kids that are just as newsworthy. I have made it my responsibility to be their self appointed spokesperson and make their remarkable accomplishments known to the masses. Until now, they have flown under the radar but all that is about to change.

The entrepreneurs you are about to meet are high achievers in various fields, but there is one major commonality between them and the young superstars they themselves admire: CReAtiviTy.

Any one of them will tell you that you need creativity to succeed, but have you really thought about what it means? Some people equate being creative with having a talent in the arts, like being gifted at drawing, writing, singing or acting. But what about those of us who prefer to paint by number or cannot carry a tune unless it is in the shower?

I prefer to think of creativity as the expression of an idea, concept or emotion through *any* outlet that you enjoy. Whether you do it through sports, mathematics, science or music is up to you.

If you think about your life up to this point, I am sure you can pinpoint times when you have needed a vehicle to get out your feelings, solve a problem or make a change. You may also notice this was about the same time you discovered you were pretty good at something. Like maybe you always knew you enjoyed sports in school, especially basketball. But one day you were exposed to tennis, and you thought, 'This is pretty cool.' Then things started happening at home; your parents were not getting along. So you found that every day you started to look forward to tennis even more because hitting that ball was a huge release for you. You started playing after school and on weekends. Little by little, your strength and skill grew and people started to comment on your "talent." You, in turn, started to feel really good and with each match you found new ways to improve your game.

CURIOSITY TO CREATIVITY TO CASH

What actually happened?

Every time you picked up that racquet you were allowing creativity to flow through you. You were giving yourself permission, without even knowing it, to channel your emotions in a constructive and positive way.

Now for some of you, it may have taken a few tries with baseball, soccer and football before you found that tennis was the one for you. We are constantly experimenting with ways to unleash our creativity and when we find the right one, it just clicks. *Our creativity causes our talents to surface.* It is amazing what happens when we tap into that inner part of ourselves and find the best way to share what we know and love with the rest of the world.

For 19-year old art prodigy, Olivia Bennett (oliviabennett. com), whose company is worth $1.5 million, her creativity was apparent at a young age but flourished when she was faced with a life changing situation.

Olivia Bennett

IN HER OWN WORDS *I have always been very creative. When I was little, I would spend hours poring over my coloring books. I think I was about four when my mom noticed that my work was pretty exceptional. Cinderella's dress was always embellished!*

Olivia Bennett

CURIOSITY TO CREATIVITY TO CASH

When I was five years old, my family moved to Salt Lake City, Utah. My mother took me in for my kindergarten checkup. The doctors noticed an abnormality in my blood tests. The doctors proceeded with several other tests; after a week, they diagnosed me with ALL (Acute Lymphoblastic Leukemia). At that point, I started intense chemotherapy and other treatments.

I went through two years' worth of treatments. One of the medications I was taking called Vincristine had a horrible effect on my hands; they became stiff and claw-like. I began physical therapy and one of my activities was painting. I was home from school during the two years of treatment. During that time I painted quite a bit. This hobby developed into a passion and release for me. I was able to get lost in my own world and express my emotions on canvas.

Now 11 years cancer-free, Olivia thoughtfully reflects on that time and actually credits her ordeal with helping her find strength and understanding that otherwise would not have been developed that early in life.

Today, Olivia's work is known nation-wide and her watercolor and oil paintings have often been compared to that of Georgia O'Keeffe. Olivia's undeniable talent is the direct result of her life experiences combined with her creativity.

But more on her later.

Do you think it requires creativity to take an existing talent and expand it into another area? You bet! It also takes courage and tenacity. Some common examples you hear are model turned actress, athlete turned television personality or lawyer turned politician. Think about when former body builder, Mr. Universe title-holder and movie action hero, Arnold Schwarzenegger, ran for and won the position of governor of California. And how amazing was it when

Bono, the lead singer of the Grammy award-winning rock band, U2, became an international humanitarian and activist?

Sometimes the move is obvious, like for 18-year old Ashley Quails, founder of <u>whateverlife.com</u>, a MySpace design company, worth $2 million.

Ashley Quails

IN HER OWN WORDS

When I was younger I loved to create. I've always loved crafts. When I got good grades in school, I wanted a craft book because my mom would say, "Well, you've got $10, what do you want to get?" So I've always just loved creative things; drawing. And so, when I was introduced to computers, it is so fun for me to see all those colors on the screen and it's really a lot of hands on and I love doing it. I love to create business cards, *create posters, things like that. So, for me to be able to create all of these graphics and all of these layouts for millions of people, essentially, it's just so fulfilling.*

I was always interested in websites, since I was around nine. And when I was about 13 or 14, my friends started using MySpace and started using all

ASHLEY QUARLS

of these different programs and they came to me because I always had been interested in graphic design. So basically I studied the code and started to make them simply for my friends. I had had personal websites, so I started posting them on my website, just, here's what I've created. I was so happy when I had one other person on the site other than me. It was a great feeling; somebody likes your art.

Ashley successfully made the move from artist to web designer simply by allowing her creativity to lead her in a new direction. She took the initiative, did her research and gave it a solid effort and found a way to broaden an existing talent into a field that thrills her even more.

But Ashley did something else, she saw a need that did not exist yet and found a way to fill it. Now that is CReAtivity!

Did Ashley know that the social networking site, MySpace, would explode the way that it did? Possibly, but what really mattered was she knew she liked what she was doing and was receiving rave reviews from her friends, who ultimately spread the word and helped her business grow. She was tuned in to her own inner guidance system and through that she was able to really see and hear what she needed to do.

What both of these young women have done is outstanding and you can follow their lead.

For many of you, the first step is to give yourself some much overdue credit. We are so hard on ourselves, focusing more on what we should not or have not done. How would your life be different if you acknowledged all that you have accomplished…even the little things? What about if you celebrated that you were on time for school for one full week, when in the past that was always a challenge for you? Or you congratulated yourself when you beat your own record at Guitar Hero®?

It may seem silly, but trust me, I give myself kudos for everyday tasks, like having a great staff meeting with my team or writing a few paragraphs of this book. Little by little, by giving yourself a pat on the back for a job well done, you are building your confidence and in return, your creative mind has more freedom to grow. It is almost as if you are giving it the go ahead to run freely and show you what it has up its sleeve!

"Hi Daddy...You know the company you told me to
get investment advice from? I just bought 'em."

©Jonny Hawkins

Professional road racing cyclist and record-breaking, seven-time winner of the Tour De France, Lance Armstrong, started his triathlete career at the age of 12. By the age of 16, he officially became a professional triathlete and at 18, he became the national sprint-course triathlon champion. As this is being written, Lance has chosen to enter his eighth Tour De France. I am cheering him on to another victory.

17

MY CHALLENGE TO YOU

For one 24-hour period, pay attention and log all of the times you do something well or think or act creatively. You can do it in your journal if you have one or in the space provided below. Guaranteed you will surprise yourself. Make sure to include things like finding a new solution to an old problem, focusing your energy on bettering yourself in an area that fills you up or doing something that just makes you or someone else smile.

CURIOSITY TO CREATIVITY TO CASH

One thing that I know for sure is that being creative means using your imagination and ingenuity to make a difference in this world. I am a great fan of Napoleon Hill's classic book, *Think and Grow Rich*. In it, he says there are two ways to use your imagination. The first way, Synthetic Imagination, is when you read, listen or think about other people's concepts, ideas or plans and find a way to improve on them. The second way is Creative Imagination, when you use old content as inspiration to pull out something totally original and brand new. Creative Imagination is when you discover your own big idea. Steve Jobs, CEO of Apple Inc., demonstrated Creative Imagination at its finest when he unveiled the iPhone with its Multi-Touch interface in 2007.

"And remember, if something should happen out of the blue—we've got you covered."

©Jonny Hawkins

We are all creative and we use this side of ourselves constantly and even unconsciously. Olivia and Ashley recognized creativity within themselves that had been there for a while and with a little extra effort, they nurtured it and let it take its shape. You will be hearing from them again further on in the book where they will reveal how they are taking their talents to the next level and sharing their gifts with others.

CHAPTER 2

PURPOSEFUL PASSION

Someone once asked me how much time I spend using my imagination. I quickly decided that was a trick question because for me, time and space disappear when I am in a creative place. I believe that spirit is working through me and I do not need to quantify the hours spent when I am at my highest and best. For me, my imagination comes alive especially when I am speaking on stage to a live audience. I feel truly guided to deliver what the audience needs and my concept of real time is gone.

There are many names for "it" but I believe, and all of the young entrepreneurs in this book agree, that "it" is your passion. Simply put, your passion is what you love to do. For Olivia Bennett, her passion is painting.

IN HER OWN WORDS

OLIVIA BENNETT

I think I was just born with this passion. I started painting seriously at age five, during my cancer treatments. Painting was such an incredible release. I was able to get lost in my own little world. When I really got into a painting, I could sit for hours and hours on end. I wasn't able to attend school during my cancer treatments, so I would spend most of the day coloring.

When I enrolled in school, my art teacher pulled my mother aside and recommended getting me into art classes. I started taking lessons and fell in love with watercolor. Up until that point I had been using Crayolas; it was fun to use the real thing! I experimented with lots of different mediums— colored pencil, pastel, charcoal, air brush—but I always went back to watercolor. This hobby soon became a passion. Cancer was really a blessing in disguise.

How many of you have a hobby that you just dabble in for fun? We touched on this in the first chapter when I said that creativity causes our talents to surface. But let us take it a step further. The key is to look at all of your talents—because there are many—and decide which one brings you the most joy. Which one, when you are fully engaged, makes time and space disappear?

What is one activity that you look forward to, lose yourself in and excel at that is your true divine imagination at work?

Wonderland Bakery (wonderlandbakery.com) in Newport Beach, California, is the product of a passion fully realized by now 23-year-old Allyson Ames. With over $2.5 million in sales, the bakery at one time was just the dream of a five-year-old little girl who loved to bake.

Allyson Ames

IN HER OWN WORDS *My inspiration and passion for baking was there as early as I can remember. I would sneak downstairs while my family was sleeping to bake and decorate.*

When I got older I couldn't wait to get home and have fun creating in the kitchen. Many of my friends would have hobbies or participate in sporting activities; however, all my free time was centered in the kitchen surrounded by my cookbooks and imagination. At 13, I had a serious cookbook collection, my wish list included a blow torch for crème brulee and my prized possession was the most beautiful aqua blue Kitchenaid stand mixer that I still use today. I was happiest when I was creating delicious and beautiful desserts for family and friends (and they were too). I knew that I'd want to attend culinary school and eventually I would want to open my dream. With divinity and hard work it all fell into place and happened a lot sooner than I had originally thought it would.

In my imagination, the concept of Wonderland would be an enchantingly delicious and

---

Fashion designer and business executive Ralph Lauren worked after school to earn money to buy suits. Best known now for his Polo by Ralph Lauren brand, he first designed and sold neck ties to his classmates.

whimsically fun place to visit. I transformed my dream into reality and now our customers, family and friends of all ages visit and enjoy any time. Seeing the reaction of customers brings me great satisfaction and drives me to share my Wonderland Bakery experience with the world.

When Allyson graduated from the International Culinary Institute at the age of 19, she already had completed a 95-page business plan for Wonderland Bakery. (Check out the bonus section of Allyson's business strategies at the back of the book.) During the six months it took to develop the plan, Allyson and her mom, who is her business partner, were immersed in it. When it came time to decide if she would further her culinary career or open her own business, she knew in her heart that the bakery was the way to go.

Amazing, right? A hobby that became her passion fueled a dream that she worked tirelessly to fulfill. Now, Wonderland Bakery has been named "Official Sweet Ambassador" for Newport Beach, is the creator of the city's official cookie, cupcake and cake, was named the "Best Gingerbread Man Cookie" in the country by Whoopi Goldberg on ABC's *The View* and has a large number of celebrity clientele. In addition, Allyson received the 2008 Business of the Year Award from California State Senator Tom Harmon and Governor Arnold Schwarzenegger for business growth and contribution to the community.

Allyson is not the only one who can turn her passion into profit.

I believe that everyone has passion. And just as creativity uncovers your talents, passion unleashes your potential.

My definition of success is the difference between where you are and the use of your full potential. Each of you has a multiplicity of talents and you need to exercise all of your potential to realize your dreams. Fair enough?

Allyson Ames

Many of us find our passion through a hobby, which is an obvious place to start. Others of us stumble upon our passion in a haphazard way when we are actually focused on something else. This is how it happened to me when I was just nine years old and my family moved to Denmark to live and learn the language, customs and traditions of that country.

During our time there I saw something that captured my young heart, mind and soul: a low handlebar racing bicycle that at the time was not available in America.

I wanted one with my entire being and could feel that I would be a great bicyclist and racer. I pretended that I owned that bicycle. I could feel it. I saw myself riding 50 miles a day to get in peak performance condition so that I could ride and compete effectively.

Every time I begged my dad for that bike he said I could buy it when I turned 21. I hammered him down to 16 and he told me not to ask again. Of course I did ask again, but this time I asked if I could have it right away if I earned it myself. My dad agreed because he was convinced there was no way I could earn that kind of money in six months time on my own. What he did not understand was how deep my desire was for that bike and how determined I was to get it.

Boy Scouts Life Magazine had an advertisement for selling greeting cards on consignment. That meant Boy Scouts gave me samples and order forms from the American Greeting Card Company. All I had to do was offer them to my neighbors and friends, collect the cash or check, send in half to the company and hand deliver the cards when they arrived. They sold for $2.00 a box and I got to keep half.

I set out on a Saturday morning and my mom gave me one main instruction: smile. Astonishingly, almost everyone I met with said yes! As you can imagine, I was very excited and in a month, I sold over 376 boxes of Christmas and greeting cards. That's $376 and for a little kid, that was big money back then. My dad had me put it all in the bank, saving half for my college fund. That was fine by me because I still had $188 for the new bike come spring.

Wanting that bicycle caused me to push myself further and develop skills sooner than I ever could have imagined. I earned my bicycle by selling and discovered early that I could sell, enjoyed selling and was good at it. That revelation would serve me magnificently to earn everything I ever wanted. Selling became my passion and my livelihood and I owe it all to that bike. I wanted it so badly that I was forced to find a way to get it using my own talents. My passion for the bike then transferred to the art of selling. I began unleashing my potential in a productive and profitable way that has served me for over 50 years.

Now I am the first one to admit that times have changed. For me to step into the world of today's youth, I had to really do my research. However, I do believe that there is one fundamental that is still the same:

When you find and live your passion, everything else falls into place.

That is how it worked out for 18-year-old Martina Butler, creator and host of emogirltalk.com, an indie music Internet radio show with over 100,000 downloads and a net worth of over $1.1 million. The weekly podcast focuses on emo, a genre of alternative rock music, but also features celebrity interviews, fashion and general topics of interest.

Martina Butler

IN HER OWN WORDS *I started my podcast Emo Girl Talk in 2005, and it started as a hobby. My dad does a podcast, so it was not really anything serious. And then about six months later, I got a sponsorship from Nature's Cure [a health and beauty company] and I was the first teen podcaster to have ever received [corporate] sponsorship.*

I really did not know that it was going to be a success. When I started doing it, it was oh, wow, I am getting a lot of listeners, a lot of feedback. And more and more sponsors started coming in. I realized I should take this a lot more seriously and I love it, but I am amazed by how much it has grown and how much it has given me.

I definitely have a career plan because of the podcast. I want to make this my career. I want to be a television host, a radio host; I want to be in business because of it. It changed my life completely.

Tyra Banks, supermodel, talk show host, actress and entrepreneur, began modeling in the 11th grade. During her first week doing runway modeling in Paris, France, she was booked for an unprecedented 25 shows, a record in the business for a newcomer!

Martina Butler

DID U KNOW?

PURPOSEFUL PASSION

Martina was the first teenager to receive a corporate sponsorship for a podcast and she continues to gain more exposure and requests from major companies including Johnson & Johnson, Kmart and Cover Girl Cosmetics. She made the decision to get serious on something that was just for fun and quickly realized all the potential that was waiting to be released. Her passion for her podcast continues to grow as she enjoys interacting with her listeners and viewers and she sees all the possibilities ahead of her.

"Never mind my throat...look after my invoices."

©Jonny Hawkins

Everything you need to find your passion is inside of you. Your true self can be seen when you are doing what you love and you then become someone others want to be around and model.

Sir Richard Branson, mega-entrepreneur and founder of the Virgin brand with over 360 companies, had his first successful business at the age of 16. Not going into business to make money, he created, edited and funded *Student Magazine*, a publication run by students, for students.

MY CHALLENGE TO YOU

Make a list of all of your interests, hobbies, school and after-school activities and volunteer work. Then circle the top three that you enjoy the most—the ones that really make your heart sing. Put the list aside and follow me to the next chapter. I have something pretty incredible to share with you.

MY HOBBIES, INTERESTS AND ACTIVITIES:

_____   _____   _____

_____   _____   _____

_____   _____   _____

_____   _____   _____

_____   _____   _____

_____   _____   _____

_____   _____   _____

_____   _____   _____

_____   _____   _____

CHAPTER 3

THE SPIRIT OF LEARNING EARNING AND RETURNING

If creativity brings our talents to the surface and passion unleashes our potential…then what happens? What do you think the next step is to bring about total transformation and success? There is a missing link and if you look closely you will start to see what it is.

Implementation!

This step is the bridge between a great idea or hobby and the next big thing. It is what makes you a Bill Gates or an Oprah Winfrey. It is what sets you apart from those who hope and those who do. Some people call it action, but I think it is more deliberate than that. Implementation is taking that idea, hobby or interest and doing something, but not just anything. It has to be movement with a purpose. Consider it your strategic plan. You want to have a reason behind every decision and act—even if that reason is that it just felt right.

Implementation is what takes you from being a dreamer to an entrepreneur. As an entrepreneur you want to expose people to ideas, concepts or products that they have never seen before. An entrepreneur is doing tomorrow's work today!

By that definition, Maryanne Barrott is most definitely an entrepreneur. She is the 18-year-old creator of the brand Maryanne's Own Bodycare Essentials (<u>maryannesown.com</u>) and the winner of the Young Entrepreneurs of America 2007 Business Plan Competition.

Maryanne Barrott

IN HER OWN WORDS *My mom works with me in the business. She helps me with it. We were both trying to think of something that we could do to stay close, since I was the last kid at home; all of my siblings had moved out.*

THE SPIRIT OF LEARNING, EARNING AND RETURNING

So it started as a summer project. We weren't really planning on turning it into a business, just something fun that we could do together. We did it at the local farmer's market where I live and pretty soon it just picked up from there. We had some people from larger farmer's markets come up to me within the second week and ask me to come and join them. And then from there it just took off. People liked the products and they started asking for more, and so it was totally unexpected.

The very first product that I made was the essential sugar scrub. I actually got that recipe from a friend and she would make them for her family just as little gifts. I got that from her, but I tweaked it and used different ingredients. For most of my other recipes I get the basis of them off of the Internet. I'll find the recipes and then I experiment with them because I always change the ingredients. I try to use more natural ingredients and I always research them to see what the benefits are and how they can help you.

We started doing markets in Sun Valley, Idaho, and that was basically all tourists. People would come and they would see our product and they would take it home with them—wherever they were going—to New York or Texas or any place. When they started to call us and still wanted the product after they had gone home, that's when I started to realize this could be a really good thing for me. That's when I made the website, the online store, so that they could buy directly off of there.

Maryanne's Own made $17,000 in revenue in 2007. With three new products introduced in 2008 and the implementation of a web marketing plan, Maryanne is taking focused and deliberate action that will result in more consistent sales per month.

Maryanne Barrott

Have you ever heard an adult say, "I wish I had done this sooner," when they reach a goal? If you think about it I am sure at least one or two people will come to mind. What about your own situation? Have you ever put off something that you knew was good for you, like getting tutored in chemistry so you could improve your grade or trying out for your school's dance team? And then when you finally did do it—aced the test and made the team—you wondered why you waited so long?

There are many theories out there about why we procrastinate on what we know is good for us, but I believe it is because we block out our inner voice. Our inner voice is there to quietly guide us, to cheer us on and to encourage us when we are afraid. Behind every great decision I have ever made, my inner voice was leading me and things just felt right. Even when I was nine years old and wanted that bike, I trusted myself and that is the moment when I first became an entrepreneur.

I did not wait. Maryanne did not wait. Olivia, Ashley, Allyson and Martina did not wait. And neither did any of the other entrepreneurs you have yet to meet. So why should you?

Start listening to yourself, right now, today. If you begin to trust yourself with smaller tasks like studying for that test instead of playing video games or raising your hand in class rather than letting someone else answer the question, bigger opportunities will begin to present themselves to you.

Maryanne knew what she liked, trusted herself and paid attention to the wants and needs of her clients. To get her sugar scrub in their hands across the country, she started her website. Now that is something!

Like Maryanne, each of the young entrepreneurs featured in this book did their first "something" to turn their passion into profit.

IN HER OWN WORDS

OLIVIA BENNETT

I was eight years old when I sold my first painting. My mom was teaching a scrapbooking workshop at our home and one of the ladies attending loved the paintings on the walls. She asked my mother who the artist was and I met her. I showed her all of my work; she was really taken with a watercolor painting of tulips. My mom and I were so shocked that she wanted to purchase one of my paintings, I told her it was $50 for the piece and she bought it. I was so excited! Within a few months, I started selling my work to teachers and neighbors. I entered my work in a few local art fairs and contests.

To date, Olivia has sold over 450 pieces of her art ranging in price from $1,500 to $20,000! She opened up her own art gallery at age 14 and ran it successfully for three years. She is currently looking for a new location. Olivia is also working on launching a clothing line based on her paintings.

IN HER OWN WORDS ASHLEY QUAILS

At the time [when she had her first website], my friends said, "This is going to be expensive, you might want to look into advertising." I was only 14 and I had never had another job other than babysitting my little sister. I started doing research on different advertising programs and that's when I signed up with Google Adsense and essentially the site just started to grow even more.

When Ashley got her first check in 2005, it was for $2,700. The next month, the check was for $10,000 and it started to gradually build to where it is now anywhere from $40,000 to $65,000 a month of steady income!

Do you see what these young women did? They did something! Not anything, but something specific that brought them closer to their goal. Olivia sold a painting to a friend instead of giving it for free. She then displayed her art in public for others to admire and purchase. Ashley took a recommendation from her peers, people she saw every day, and began researching ways to financially support her site. Then she ultimately chose the one that best suited her needs and watched as the money started to roll in and her business grew.

Ashley, Olivia and all of the entrepreneurs in this book are focused on financial independence. They are excited to know that their creativity, good thinking and intellectual property can turn into money now. In turn they can help their peers, family, school and community become free of debt and stress. They are sharing their high ideals and values because if we keep thinking, protecting, sharing and selling our ideas, the economy will be infinitely sustainable and expandable.

"I could get off the ground if not for the start-up costs."

©Jonny Hawkins

MY CHALLENGE TO YOU

Look back at the list you made from the previous chapter, where you circled your top three hobbies or activities. Ask yourself this question *for each one:*

If this hobby of _____ brings me so much joy, how can I share it with others in a way that has never been done before and earn or create a profitable enterprise?

_____

_____

_____

If this hobby of _____ brings me so much joy, how can I share it with others in a way that has never been done before and earn or create a profitable enterprise?

_____

_____

_____

If this hobby of _____ brings me so much joy, how can I share it with others in a way that has never been done before and earn or create a profitable enterprise?

_____

_____

_____

DID U KNOW?

THE SPIRIT OF LEARNING, EARNING AND RETURNING

Read this question before you go to sleep. Say it when you wake up in the morning. Ponder it while you walk your dog. I guarantee the answer, if not immediately apparent, will show itself to you.

Be aware of your surroundings and the people that you meet. Even if you think every day is the same—you go to the same places, you see the same people—the more familiar you are with your environment, the more likely you are to notice when something new appears, no matter how subtle it is.

In some ways, you want to be like Adrian Monk, the quirky detective on the hit television series *Monk*, who has an attention to detail that few possess. With a razor-sharp focus and unmatched skill of observation, he is able to pick up on small inconsistencies, identify patterns and connect the clues that usually lead to solving the crime. It is not about becoming a super sleuth; it is about locating and using your inner Monk to expand your awareness in your daily life.

Do you think the entrepreneurs in this book trust themselves? Yes! Do you think they have doubts? Yes! Do you think it is always easy? No way! Being an entrepreneur means trusting yourself even when others do not, when the next step is not so clear and when it really is the last thing you feel like doing.

Nathan Nguyen is a 22-year-old online retailer whose company, Instrumental Savings, Inc. (instrumentalsavings.com), a musical instrument retailer and distributor, sold over $1.4 million in 2007. Nathan has always trusted his gut, paid attention to his environment and taken every opportunity to implement what he has learned. A Horatio Alger award winner (horatioalger.org), Nathan attended one of my Mega seminars during his senior year of high school. Inspired by what he learned there, he made a major decision before going off to college the next year.

Bill Gates, chairman of Microsoft Corporation, discovered his interest in software and began programming computers at the age of 13. By his junior year at Harvard University, he knew the life-changing importance of the computer and began developing software for personal computers.

39

Nathan Nguyen

IN HIS OWN WORDS *I said the four years that I have in college will be the only four years that I will have the time to build a business because upon graduation there will be a lot of financial pressure.*

There will be a lot of pressure to get a job and earn money. So I made a commitment to leverage those four years to make all the mistakes and build as many businesses as I can and learn as much as I can by doing and applying what my professors teach immediately.

Nathan ventured into real estate and his first transaction was helping his sister buy a property, the family's first real-estate investment ever. This gave him confidence that when he applied what he learned, it would work. After time went by and lessons were learned, he made a huge realization—he was living in a globalization age, which he describes as a time when the globe is coming together, working together. Still wanting to leverage his time while he was in college, he decided on retail as it seemed to be the most logical place to start and the most convenient; he could do it online right from his apartment. But what is most interesting to me—and I hope to you—is how he found his product.

IN HIS OWN WORDS NATHAN NGUYEN

I always joked around with my roommate. I said "You are the perfect consumer because you just like to buy stuff." I am a pretty frugal guy because doing business you have to save every penny you can get. So one day

THE SPIRIT OF LEARNING, EARNING AND RETURNING

I walked home from my class thinking, 'What am I going to sell?' And he walked in with a package and I asked, "What did you just buy today?" He bought a guitar!

I do not play music. I do not know how to play any instrument, but I know that my roommate has a guitar and he is a student and if I can get millions of customers like my roommate then I will be okay. So I went towards the industry of musical instruments in the summer of 2006 and I have been doing that ever since. It was that guitar that sparked it all...so I couldn't have started this business without my roommate's inspiration. That is it. That is how the journey starts.

Nathan's business was right under his nose the whole time but it was not until he was really ready to believe in himself and his capabilities that he found it. He is a true entrepreneur in the sense that his goal is to bring value to himself, his family, his customers, his clients, his future and his world.

nathan nguyen

He sums up this chapter perfectly:

IN HIS OWN WORDS

NATHAN NGUYEN

It is not how much information you have in order to start a business. It is how much effort and persistence you have, because knowledge and information gets compounded by execution and action.

Implementation—easy as that!

SUPERSTAR
at a Glance

CAMERON JOHNSON

Age 24
President, Cameron Johnson Inc.
Net Worth: Undisclosed (Private Companies)
cameronjohnson.com

Cameron Johnson had 12 businesses before he was
21. Every single one of them was on the Internet.

How did you first get into business?

I started my first business when I was nine years old.
It was a small printing company called, Cheers &
Tears Printing Company and I printed greeting cards,
stationery, anything that I could print with my computer
and printer. I ran that business for several years.

I got my first checking account when I was 10 years
old. My parents tried to help teach me the importance
of saving money and financial literacy. And when I
was 12 years old I started selling Beanie Babies over
the Internet. That year, for my 13th birthday, I made
$50,000 profit selling Beanie Babies through a website
that I started and also on eBay and everywhere else that
I could sell them. I became one of the biggest online
retailers of Beanie Babies and I had a website called,
Beanie Wholesale and we would sell to retailers across
the country and we would sell to consumers around the
world.

At our peak, I was shipping 40 orders a day and I was
stocking 5,000 Beanie Babies in a closet in my parents'
basement that I would pay $75 a month rent for to use
that closet. And every day after school I would come
home; I would get all the orders from the night before,
because before I'd go to bed I would make all the
orders and box them all up and print the labels and
have all the invoices done. My mom would take me to
the post office on my way to soccer practice—
I played soccer throughout high school and I played

for 13 years—and then at the end of the night I would come home and do the exact same thing and repeat the whole process. So that was my business when I was 12 and 13.

When I was 15, I got into an online advertising company that I started called SurfingPrizes.com and that company I launched with two other teenagers. We were placing 15 million ads per day in just our first six months of operation. When we were doing 15 million ads we had 200,000 customers and we were generating $15,000 per day in revenue.

When I was 17, I owned an Internet company called, Emazing Sites. And what Emazing Sites did was we were a holding company for several large web properties, one called, InternetProfiles.com. I had my hands in a lot of different businesses. At the time we had a web design firm where we would design websites for different companies. I ran that for several years until ultimately I closed it.

I went off to college. I went to Virginia Tech. And when I was at Virginia Tech I started a company, my first semester there, called, Certificate Swap. 80 percent of Americans either buy or receive a gift card and my idea was to have an outlet where you can get rid of the gift cards you don't want. So what CertificateSwap.com enabled you to do was you would come onto our web site and you would list your gift card for sale. Say you had $100 value; you would list it for sale for say, $85. Meanwhile, someone else is happy to buy that $100 certificate for $85 and you're happy to get $85 cash that you can spend anywhere. So we just connected

buyers and sellers, much like eBay. I left college and raised venture capital for that company and ultimately turned down a $10 million venture capital offer because of some of the contingencies. I moved on and my partner and I sold it and we made a really nice return in just several months of operating that business. That was my business when I was 19. There were several more that I skipped over.

You said your parents had you save. How much did they ask you to save?

The first thing they taught me to do was to tithe to the church. I always gave 10 percent of everything that I made to the church. I started writing checks to the church when I was 10 years old after I got that first account. As for savings, one of the best things about starting a business when you still live with your parents or when you're still in school is that your expenses are very, very minimal. What does a 12-year-old spend any amount of money on? I might spend money going to the movies or something like that. It wasn't a conversation that my parents really had to have with me as far as saving because I never wanted to spend money. I couldn't drive for another six years so I wasn't spending money on ridiculous things. I couldn't take trips by myself. I wasn't buying fancy clothes. I was just a normal kid.

What really got me interested in saving though was when I was 11 years old and I had the checking account for a year. It was Christmas time and when I came downstairs to see what Santa brought me, I opened up my stocking and inside my stocking were three rolled up stock certificates. What my parents had done was they bought me one share of stock in three companies that I knew. So they bought me Marriott Hotels, CSX Railroad and Walt Disney Corporation. These stocks all traded for $20 to $30, so this gift, one share of each of these companies cost them less than $100, yet that instantly got me interested in the stock market. And that's where I started saving my money and that's where I started investing my money. I did quite well in the stock market after that. I started a Roth IRA retirement account when I was 14 and I started putting away money for the long term.

I've always been putting money away for retirement simply because the younger you start on your retirement, every dollar you save is exponentially more than that because it has so much time to appreciate. And the difference between starting even at age 20 versus age 30 is exponentially greater. So many people want to delay that and most people don't even start thinking about their retirement until they are in their mid to late 30s, maybe even 40s, and that's not too late obviously, it's never too late, but it's so much more beneficial to start at a very early age. That's probably one of the smartest things I ever did was to save money instead of spend it when I was younger because that's a certain something that I'll have to be thankful for way down the road.

Did you spend money on computers and software yourself?

When I was nine years old I was one of the last kids on the block to get a computer and I got it for Christmas.

I got the computer and printer and I felt like I was playing catch up. And what I did was, I started the printing business, but with the profits of that business I went in and reinvested in equipment. I've always been reinvesting my money into my own equipment so that I could print better products for my customers and also just have the latest and greatest technologies. I've always tried to save and everything I really bought has been something that I earned myself. It's self-rewarding to know that I've been able to be self-sufficient since I was in the ninth grade.

What do you recommend for the leapfrog way of catching up?

We live in a generation where "I don't know" isn't a sufficient answer because we all have access to the Internet and we have access to the answers to all of our questions. I happen to be one who is self-taught. I started reading business magazines when I was really young to learn about business. I started teaching myself everything about how the Internet worked and how to start businesses. To this day, I cannot design a website, I don't know programming and a lot of people get discouraged because they say, "Well, I don't know how to do that or I don't know how to do this." Well, I don't either and one of my talents is to be able to **find the people who can complement my skills and who can do the things that I can't do, because together we can all do great things.**

How did you figure out how to make money on the Internet?

Anytime I would come up with an idea I would write

it down and then later I would do research on that idea to see if (1) that idea already exists and (2) if it doesn't exist how can I create it and bring it to market and monetize it? And if it does already exist, is that company making money? **Just because it already exists, that shouldn't discourage you from your idea.** Competition is a beautiful thing. So if something already exists, that's actually validation for your idea. That means you're actually on to something and then maybe there's a way you can make it better or cheaper or faster or easier.

All these Internet companies might have big revenues or they might have millions of users but they don't actually make a profit. All of my businesses were profitable but that was because they were much smaller. **I always believed in starting small.** I always believed in investing my own money, not taking on outside investments and starting with literally, sometimes $50, sometimes $500, never more than several thousand dollars to start any of my businesses. So it's something that can be duplicated because even though I did raise money and was offered venture capital for one of my companies, I turned it down.

Never taken on millions of dollars. I've never taken on any loans. I've never taken on any debt and I've always started small. And everything has been a stepping stone, every business has just been a little bit bigger than the previous business and I think that's what helped me be successful. And even though I'm 24 today, I made a million dollars before I was out of high school and it also didn't happen overnight. I had been doing it for a long time and now at this point I've been

doing it 15 years, so the better part of my life has been dedicated to my businesses and that's obviously why I am where I am today.

What are the questions you ask yourself to figure out a business?

I think a lot of people, when they come up with an idea, they're afraid to share it. And they come to me all the time and they say, who should I tell my idea to? How do I know if it's a good idea? Well, I take the exact opposite approach. **I actually share my idea with lots of people and I get their immediate feedback.** They're not going to go out and steal my idea. It just hasn't happened yet. And obviously if you're that worried about it you can get them to sign a non-disclosure agreement or something else to protect you. So I look for instant responses and gratification from my friends and my family and business partners as to what they think of the idea.

But second, I go out and I look and see if the idea already exists and if it does then I look to see how I can make it better, how can I make it faster, why does this company not work or maybe why does this company do really well and how can I compete with that and take a piece of what they're doing. I wouldn't say that it's a direct formula of ABC but it's definitely a weird science that I believe in finding out all the information you possibly can and knowing your competitors better than they know themselves. **I want to know everything about my competition and sometimes just having a new set of eyes is what helps create a new business.**

Is being successful in business in your genes or is it that you have the self-initiative?

I think I always idolized my parents or realized that I was going to be like them one day. I was going to go into the business world and I think I realized that I wanted to be on their side of the desk. I wanted to be someone in charge. I wanted to be a manager. I wanted to be the owner of a business. I wanted to be an entrepreneur just like they were. And that's what I think inspired me first of all to get started really young.

I think I had the tenacity to want to be like my parents but also to be like some of my idols like Donald Trump, Michael Dell, Richard Branson, Bill Gates. I looked at all those people and I said, "Hey, if they can do it why can't I?" I looked at Michael Dell and Bill Gates and they started when they were in college. I looked at Richard Branson who started when he was in high school. I wanted to be just like these people.

My parents never pushed me into business. At the time my parents knew nothing about the Internet and very few people actually knew about the Internet. I grew up with the Internet and there wasn't anyone out there who had more experience on the Internet than I did because it just happened to be my timing. So just because I was nine or 10 years old and I had been using the Internet for two years, even if I was someone with an MBA and I was 27 years old working for Microsoft, they had only been on the Internet a few years. **I think the Internet makes it an equal playing field. It doesn't matter if you're in college or if you're in India, it's an equal playing field and you have access to the same customers** and that's the beauty of the new global economy that we live in.

Do you have other mentors other than your parents?

I met some successful people over the years. A close mentor of mine was a guy by the name of Richard Rossi. He runs a huge company called, Envision EMI where high-achieving young people come to his program every year. And I got to meet him when I was 17 and he was putting on an event where Michael Dell was going to be the keynote speaker. He had hired me and invited me to be the other keynote speaker. Michael Dell was an idol to me so I got to share the stage with Mr. Dell. And then Richard ended up being a mentor to me and he still is a mentor to me to this day. I consider you a mentor to me. Everyone around me, who I look up to, I look to as mentors. **A mentor doesn't have to be someone you have coffee with every Thursday. A mentor can be someone who you appreciate and you look up to and you study through their books and through their teachings** and that's definitely what I believe.

What are your passionate purposes right now?

My two passions right now revolve around education. One is high-school dropout rates, so I serve on the board of an organization called, Jobs for America's Graduates. And they identify ninth graders who are potentially going to drop out of high school and they put them into our specialized program. It's in 39 states and we have a 90 percent retention rate. I'm passionate about keeping people in school because I believe if you don't educate now then you're going to incarcerate later. I think education is really important at the high-school level.

The other piece of education that I'm really passionate about is financial literacy because I didn't realize this at the time, but I was really fortunate to get a financial literacy education from my parents from that first checking account to the stock certificates and other things that no other kids or very few are fortunate enough to get. I think financial literacy is something that we're going to have to institute in the schools because that's something that affects people in the real world and in many cases it's more important than almost any other subject.

What are the key points that you want everybody to have for financial literacy?

The biggest thing is it's fascinating that you can be 18 years old, you can graduate high school, you can go off to college and you can get a credit card with a $5,000 limit and you can sign up for as much student loans as you can possibly imagine, but you've never even been taught to balance a checkbook; you've never been taught how to manage a savings account. The only thing you've been taught to do is to maybe work and if you do work and then cash the paycheck and spend it, that's terrible. You've got to learn how to save, learn how to give and help the country and help those in need.

What is your model for charitable contribution?

I went into this with a scientific model. I'm introduced to so many charities almost on a weekly basis. I'm passionate about the ones I support and I try to have a personal involvement. It's not just a matter of writing a check. I like to be really active and whether it's bringing recognition to the charity or whether it's serving on their board, I want to be really involved in actually creating material and getting it out there.

What has been the highlight of your young career?

I've been really fortunate that it's kind of been a fun journey and my motto has always been, "What's next?" So I'm always just excited about what's around the corner and what I haven't done, not so much what I have done. So I'm proud of my accomplishments and being a part of *Oprah's Big Give*, traveling the country and helping people in need and seeing it first-hand. And then also the charities that I support, also the financial success I've been able to have through my businesses that has helped create products and services that have helped other businesses and helped other customers and helped employees. It's just the American dream and I've certainly lived it.

What is your most important rule of business?

My most important rule of business is having a plan.

What is the role of technology in the future of entrepreneurship?

The beauty of IT is that it lets all of us compete on an equal platform. Think about where we would be without the cell phone. Think about how much that has progressed business. Think about what email has done. Think about the way you can now virtualize your company and you can have an 800 number and that 800 number can ring into voice mail and those voice mails can be sent to you on email. This is how I operate. I have an 800 number for my office and the voice mails come straight to my computer as an email file, as a sound file, so I can be on the beach in Cancun listening to my voice mail, running my business and I don't need to be paying an office building. I don't need to have manufacturing. I don't need to have anything.

What is the most important chapter of your book *You Call the Shots*?

The very first chapter and it's called, "Put Yourself Out There." Because you can have great ideas, you can be a brilliant person, you can get all the education you want, you can have all the connections you want, but if you don't actually take the first step to follow through then nothing else matters.

What would you say to other young entrepreneurs to inspire them to live their dreams?

I would say to keep it up. We need more people that can do it.

What percentage of kids do you think have entrepreneurial tendencies?

I would say it's very, very close to 100 percent. Entrepreneurship is all around young people. What percentage of Girl Scouts sell cookies? 100 percent. What percentage of schools do fundraisers selling wrapping paper or gifts? 100 percent of schools do that. What percentage of Boy Scouts sell popcorn? What percentage of kids do lemonade stands? **Entrepreneurship is not taught, but it happens everywhere around young people and as long as they take it to the next level, which is what the Internet enables you to do and it certainly enabled me to do, then everyone can be an entrepreneur and everyone is an entrepreneur.**

MAKING IT WORK

CHAPTER 4

TURN PROBLEMS INTO PROFITS

I have made a special point of mentioning creativity in every chapter because I want to expand your awareness of it in the short amount of time that we have together. I cannot emphasize enough the importance of understanding and utilizing this valuable resource within you. It is always there, waiting to be called upon to handle any situation…especially the tough ones… it just loves those!

Problems have been called many things—bumps on the road, hiccups, detours or setbacks—just to name a few. But what if you thought of problems in a whole new way? What if problems are opportunities? What if around the corner from your next big problem was your next big solution?

That is exactly how it worked out for 17-year-old Jasmine Lawrence, owner of EDEN Body Works (edenbodyworks.com), a natural hair and skin care products company worth $3 million.

Jasmine Lawrence

IN HER OWN WORDS *I was 11 years old when I got a relaxer put in my hair and the damage from the chemicals in the relaxer caused almost all of my hair to break off.*

It was really traumatic and devastating for me. I didn't know what to do. I was only 11 years old and being a girl, my hair and the way I looked meant everything to me. So just losing that stopped me in my tracks. I used to be really outgoing and talkative and after that I was really shut in and I didn't want anybody to see me. I was really embarrassed about the way I looked and I was shy. That just wasn't who I am.

So I started looking for all-natural products that I could use, things that wouldn't have chemicals that would hurt me again. My parents and I started looking at different stores, online, we went to different doctors and I just couldn't find anything that would really work for me. So I started looking at the old shampoo and conditioner bottles and things like that, that I had lying around my house that I refused to use. I started looking on the back of those and started looking up those long chemical names they had on there and what they were used for. I thought to myself, 'There has to be something else that you can use.' We didn't always have chemicals. People were washing their hair before all this stuff was put together.

I started looking up all-natural alternatives to those chemicals and I found information in books, online, and I'm actually still finding information now. People are sending me books for all-natural herbs; not just for your hair, but for your food and different things like that. It really grew on me. I saved up my allowance, got my parents' permission, went online and started ordering these all-natural ingredients. I didn't know what I was going to do with them at first. I just started mixing them together to see what would happen, how it smelled, how it felt in my hand and eventually I developed the all-natural hair oil and it really helped grow back my hair. I started giving it to my friends and my family to see how they liked it, and right then and there it was really just a family secret. It wasn't something that I was planning on expanding and growing until I was about 13 years old and I went to a business camp. At the business camp they taught me all about being an entrepreneur, they taught me how to be my own boss, and that you could really make a difference if you just have an idea and run with it.

Jasmine's story really touches me because here is a young woman entering a period of her life when self esteem is so critical and instead of wallowing, she took control and designed a product that smelled good, felt good and actually did what it was intended to do: it started growing the hair! Her very personal problem became an opportunity for her to create change on a larger scale and she did. Her natural hair and skin care products are being carried in many nationwide retailers including Wal-Mart and Whole Foods Market.

JASMINE *Lawrence*

Since problems are opportunities, would you agree that more often than not, they can be positive experiences? A problem is just a solution that has not yet been discovered! It is an opportunity for either personal growth or public awareness. It is a chance to give people a resource that they may not even know they need. What matters most is being the first one to notice what is missing and then find the way to close the gap.

Twenty-year-old Chauncey Holloman is the CEO of Harlem Lyrics (officialharlem-lyrics.com), a hip-hop greeting card company worth $1.2 million.

Chauncey Holloman

IN HER OWN WORDS *The idea for the concept [greeting cards] came to me when I was shopping for a greeting card for a really close friend of mine, my best friend actually.*

She was a girl and I wanted a special card because she was turning 16 and I wanted something to say exactly how much she meant to me and exactly how close we were. I went from card to card and they were either way too mature with a very, very adult mindset or they were very, very immature. So I came to my mom that night and told her that this is a huge gap in greeting cards. There are no greeting cards specifically for teenagers and especially urban teenagers. She told me that this sounded like a good idea and a good concept and she told me to submit to her a business plan. I was 15 at that time, so of course I did not know what a business plan was but I looked up the definition and I handed it to her. It is pretty much how Harlem Lyrics got started.

Chauncey was able to see the bigger picture when dealing with this opportunity. She was not finding what she needed or wanted as a consumer and this was a problem to her and she figured to other teenagers as well. Looking at it from the perspective of wanting to solve it, she had her big idea moment. She became the solution.

I have heard many people say, "I had that same idea," when a new problem-solving concept, product or business is revealed to the public. And I always say, "I am sure you did. But you continued to let it be a problem. Why is that?" Most people will come up with a list of excuses and I just chuckle to myself because I know first hand what it takes to be an enlightened thinker and problem solver.

Many of you may know that I co-founded the bestselling *Chicken Soup for the Soul* series with Jack Canfield; some of you may even have bought or received one of our books as a gift. Most recently we published *Chicken Soup for the American Idol Soul* and it has become one of our most popular editions. But what you may not realize is that we had to fight for the first book, which at the time was a concept that we thought the public really needed. Our purpose for

the book was to change the world one story at a time. We wanted to have heart-touching and soul-penetrating stories that were soothing like a warm bowl of chicken soup.

As it happens in many businesses, we were not met with the warm welcome we had expected. Over the course of three years, 144 publishers turned down the book; they would not publish it. But I would

Emmy Award-nominated television and radio host, television producer, entrepreneur and entertainment mogul Ryan Seacrest began his broadcasting career by hosting the morning announcements at his high school. Long before becoming the host of the phenomenon *American Idol,* he had his first radio internship at the age of 15 and his first television appearance at 18.

67

not quit! I knew that people needed this book, that it was more than a compilation of stories; it had spirit. Fortunately, the 145th publisher said yes and the book was published. One and a half years later, it made it to number one on *The New York Times* bestsellers list and now the *Chicken Soup* series has 200 titles in print, 144 million books sold and is translated in 41 different languages.

I tell you this story because the most common problem you will face when you begin your business is what I and so many others have had to deal with, rejection. But if you spin it around and look at it as an opportunity, rejection is merely a challenge for you to find a better way. It is a chance for you to make a slight shift or change in your approach or to realign yourself with your product, business or service so that everyone will feel your passion and purpose. All it takes is one yes, when all you have been hearing is no, for your confidence to soar!

"I'd like an upgrade, please."

©Jonny Hawkins

TURN PROBLEMS INTO PROFITS

IN HER OWN WORDS

JASMINE LAWRENCE

I started with my oil and I basically went from salon to salon with a little rolling cart of oil and I asked, "Hey, would you like to try my product," and I told them all a little bit about my company and why I started. A lot of people said no; they laughed in my face; they stared at me like I was a joke or something and it really made me upset. It really disheartened me from wanting to do this business but my parents encouraged me. For months I would be really on fire because of business and then other months the business would be slow. I wouldn't be so happy about it but I kept working on my label designs, I kept working on my bottles, kept working on the formulas and things got better. A salon eventually said yes, then another one said yes and things started moving along.

Then I started to be asked for different products, shampoos, conditioners, lots of different things. I wanted to develop more products but I definitely needed more revenue to make that happen. I launched a website in 2006 and I started selling online on my website and I started doing different exposés and full career days at different colleges to try to get the word out about my business, about entrepreneurship. It really helped me learn a lot about networking and getting to know people, voicing my opinions, my ideas, and that helped to bring a lot of traffic to the website. So basically by word of mouth, it spread.

My great friend Wyland, the Michelangelo of the sea, started painting when he was very young, at the age of three. Because he was born with a club foot, he was limited in his physical activity. While he was stuck sitting at home, he imagined what it would be like to become Jacque Costeau or Llyod Bridges, the actor on the TV show *Sea Hunt*. Living in Michigan, the only way he could transcend his surroundings was to use his imagination through his art, oil on canvass. Wyland's mom was a hard-working, single mom with four boys and she struggled to make ends meet. Fortunately, Wy had 11 operations to straighten his club foot, paid for by the March of Dimes, an organization for which he later raised a lot of money.

Wyland was the green artist for the 2008 Beijing Olympics, where he had three children from every country from Afghanistan to Zimbabwe help him paint a three-mile canvas called, Hands Across the Ocean. Wyland wants every young person to awaken their artist and full talents within. The Wyland Foundation is dedicated to making every drop of water a clean drop. Frequently, we see young people turn their adversities into profitable advantages and make their lemons into profitable lemonade.

Jasmine persevered and showed just how determined she was to succeed. Her passion for her product meant more to her than the rejection she faced. She knew that her product could and would change lives and it was that mindset that kept her going. As famous American film director Woody Allen said, "80 percent of success is showing up." The same day Jasmine lost a Black Enterprise Teenpreneur competition, she was approached by a Wal-Mart representative and given the chance of a lifetime. She continues to strive to meet the needs of her diverse multicultural customers and is currently expanding her product line to do just that.

So do you understand how problems are a necessary part of life? That when you view them as opportunities they make us stronger, healthier and happier? I have lived my life according to the words of one of my heroes, Dr. Norman Vincent Peale. He wrote a book called *The Power of Positive Thinking* and he said, "Every problem has in it the seeds of its own solution. If you don't have any problems, you don't get any seeds." He also is known for saying that problems are good and the only people without problems are in the graveyard.

MY CHALLENGE TO YOU

Think about the role problems play in your life. Are they the main character? Are you constantly talking about what is wrong instead of what you can do to make it right? Listen to your language and that of your friends, family and even the people on your favorite television shows. When you hear the word problem—from anyone, even yourself—make a mental switch and say out loud, "Opportunity." Pretty soon it will become habit and you will start to see things as they really are.

You are bigger than your problems. You are never given a problem that you cannot personally solve or find someone who can solve it with you if you truly want a solution. And if there is one thing you can count on, it is that one problem leads to another. How about that? One opportunity leads to another! And how you handle each and every opportunity is what sets you apart from the people who make excuses and those that impact lives.

Ephren Taylor may not be a kid anymore at the age of 25, but I knew he had to be a part of this book because of all that he has accomplished. His first major move as an entrepreneur was developing video games at the young age of 12. At 16, he raised over $250,000 from investors to build an online job search engine for teens and college students, valued at over $3.4 million. At 19 he financed yet another new company, COC Ventures, a faith-based initiative that focused on creating dramatic financial returns for church congregations through community real-estate investments.

After a short-lived retirement, Ephren became the youngest African-American CEO of a publicly held company, City Capital Corp (citycapitalcorp.net), an investments and holdings company that builds value for investors and shareholders through "socially-conscious investing to empower urban communities." But this incredible journey was not always easy.

Ephren Taylor

I started at the age of 12 because I couldn't afford video games. So, basically my mom encouraged me to go out and make my own.

I was able to accomplish that goal and actually started creating my own games. Then by the time I got to the eighth grade I started making websites on the Internet. And you know everybody has that story if they're in technology. But what I learned very early on, it's a fortunate lesson, was that I was on the wrong side of the equation.

After that I just went totally towards ownership. I had a series of failures, failure after failure of trying to start my own company. But I was resilient, kept with it. So by the time I got to high school I created a dot com concept that was funded for about $750,000, [and had] about 13 employees including my high school history teacher who actually quit his job and was working for me. They said our company was about $3.5 million, but I left it because I believe that the company and some of the investors were taking it in a direction that I didn't exactly prescribe to.

I left all that I had behind, the money, the stock and everything. I went out to start another consulting firm that one of my mentors did very well. In 90 days that company was actually larger than my original company. I sold it; retired. Came out of retirement and started doing good by actually going into urban communities, helping them revitalize areas, creating affordable housing and dealing with a lot of the social and cultural issues that we face.

When you speak with Ephren, he is very clear that persistence and resilience are what kept him going forward even when he had to start over more than once. And because of that he is in a position to create positive change and self-sufficiency for communities around the world. A published author and speaker, Ephren has been spreading his message of possibility; his latest outlet for reaching the youth of today is through his Millionaire Lifestyle Institute (themillionairelifestyle.com), a success and wealth mentoring program. You can also catch a daily dose of Ephren on youtube.com.

EPHREN TAYLOR

Ephren's made his life work about being the solution and he will be the first to tell you that the payoff is more than financial wealth. When you find a way to meet the needs of others, you are rewarded in more ways than you can count. Olivia Bennett also believes the same thing:

IN HER OWN WORDS

OLIVIA BENNETT

I think it is important to look at every challenge that comes your way as an opportunity to rise up, grow, to learn more about yourself and to be a much stronger person. It is possible for people to overcome huge obstacles; we just have to believe that we can. Sometimes we are faced with things that are truly awful, but it is important that we stand strong and visualize ourselves living out the life we want to live. I have endured some things in my life so that I can reach out to others who are in need. If I can convey something that inspires them then it's all worth it!

Enough said.

CHAPTER 5

GROW RICH IN YOUR NICHE

One of my goals for this book is for you to see a bit of yourself in these entrepreneurs. They range in age, background, interests and personalities and I know that at least one of them will make a lasting impression on you, if not all.

Out of the nine outstanding entrepreneurs you have met so far, is there one story that is speaking to you louder than the others? Is there one person that you identify with more so than the rest? Take a few minutes to think about Olivia, Ashley, Martina, Allyson, Maryanne, Nathan, Jasmine, Chauncey and Ephren. Out of these superstars, whose vision is closest to yours? Who can you relate to the most in terms of what industry they are in and what product or service they are providing?

In answering these questions, you are identifying what you like and perhaps, starting to see your own path begin to take shape. It may be overwhelming for you but just remember that these kids used what they liked to find their place in the market. Not only did they use what they liked, they trusted that others would like it as much as them.

"Those are my neighbors...otherwise known as my
'target market'."

©Jonny Hawkins

Your target market is also known as your niche, the group where your concept, product or service will have the most appeal. In my professional life I am known for saying, *"Grow rich in your niche through total market penetration."* What this basically means is, find your audience and give them everything they need and want before they even know they need and want it.

Who is your audience? If you have not discovered your big idea, narrowing your market, those you want to serve, may be just the direction you need to take.

Chelsea Eubank is the 21-year old CEO of Faithful Fish® (`faithfulfish.com`), a Christian-based clothing line worth $1 million. Her concept of designer clothing for the faithful came about after a series of tragic losses including the death of her father when she was just 17. Chelsea wanted to show the joy of her faith in a subtle, not in-your-face kind of way. She decided that there was nothing on the market that appealed to her.

Chelsea Eubank

IN HER OWN WORDS *Something inspired me to draw out what I would like to wear and I showed my mom my drawings. From that moment I realized that I wanted to create a Christian line of clothing that we could be proud to wear—*

a line of clothing that showed our faith and allowed people to wear who they are on their heart. I started a clothing company...with our main mission to tithe a portion of our profits to Christian charities.

CHELSEA EUBANK

In dealing with her heartache, Chelsea also discovered an untouched niche, fashion-forward teens and young adults who are proud of their faith.

We mentioned Maryanne Barrott earlier with her company, Maryanne's Own Bodycare Essentials. Her original niche was tourists in search of unique products, but the launch of her website has allowed a greater number of consumers to find her.

IN HER OWN WORDS

MARYANNE BARROTT

We have people from everywhere and that's from all the tourists that came in to buy a product. Then they go back home and they keep ordering off the website and they tell their friends about it. So their friends get on the website and order from us.

Having good quality products to actually help people is really important to me. So doing all the research—all the ingredients that I use—I know exactly what I am doing and how it is helping people.

Maryanne was lucky in that she did not have to ask her market what they wanted; they told her! They reached out to her and she answered. Because of her efforts, her Maryanne's Own product line, featuring scrubs, lotions, body washes, a chocolate spa care line and a mineral makeup line, are being stocked in households nationwide.

Chauncey Holloman lets you know her target audience right away on her website with the words: *Hip-Hop is more than Music*. She found a way to jump in and use her fresh ideas to expand an already thriving market.

IN HER OWN WORDS CHAUNCEY HOLLOMAN

One of my advantages...is that I am so young. It is a fact that people want to see more from my generation. That gave me a bit of an advantage and the fact that the greeting card line itself is so bright; it is so vibrant; it is so urban. It is so my generation that I had this wide-open enormous niche that was completely untouched.

With an initial launch of eight cards funded by her mom's tax refund, Chauncey won an entrepreneurial competition as well as $10,000 in startup money. Since then she has created over 70 cards that are available in 13 states. She has even set her sights higher with a brand new line of clothing, based on the characters on her cards. Her HoodTees display affirmations for teen girls that Chauncey says are truly the essence of hip hop.

Liz Claiborne, fashion designer who invented a unique style of women's work clothing, entered the Jacques Heim National Design Contest advertised in Harper's *Bazaar* Magazine at the age of 19. She submitted a sketch of a woman's coat and won a ten-day trip to Paris.

Jasmine Lawrence reaches a broad target market since her EDEN Body Works line is being carried in Wal-Mart. The initial 10-store order was for a whopping 60,000 units. When that test run was a success, Jasmine's line got placed in another 270 stores across the country! And although her contract with Wal-Mart is still in effect, she also wants to cater to her smaller niche of those who specifically seek out natural hair and skin products.

IN HER OWN WORDS   JASMINE LAWRENCE

I wanted my product to be affordable for people. I wanted it to be accessible for everyone. So going into Wal-Mart was really great because a lot of people shop there and a lot of people see they have great prices.

Whole Foods is actually starting my aromatherapy line—candles and bath salts and they're in handmade wooden jars. They have more of that earthy tone and Whole Foods is an extremely natural store that I'm really starting to target, not just mass-market places but select stores, just specialty stores to be able to offer those to people who are already looking for natural products.

Ashley Quails appeals to Internet savvy teens and adults and so does Martina Butler. Come to think of it, all of the entrepreneurs you have met and the ones still to come are using technology to reach and increase their target market.

Internet usage around the world has quadrupled since the year 2000, with over 248 million people online in the United States alone (<u>internetworldstats.com</u>). We read online, communicate online, connect with others online and buy online. And what we buy ranges from books to clothing to you name it! But what you may have already picked up on is that you do not necessarily have to sell to make money online.

Like Ashley Quail, whose offerings on her website are completely

"Billy can't come out to play right now —
his baseball card business is about to go
Global."

©Jonny Hawkins

free, Martina Butler's site is totally free as well. Both young women
are compensated through sponsorships and advertising. Big companies pay these women to advertise on their sites! Why? Because they
know that Ashley and Martina have the attention of their target
audience—the same one that they want, simple as that.

Mark Zuckerberg is a young entrepreneur and computer program-
mer whose name you may not recognize, but I am willing to bet you
are familiar with his website. In 2004, from his dorm room at Harvard University, Mark created the social networking site Facebook.
At first it was for Harvard students only, but in a few short months,
with the help of his roommates, the website expanded to 45 schools

and hundreds of thousands of users. From there it grew to include anyone and everyone and in 2008 Facebook had 66 million active users, estimated annual sales of $150 million and Mark himself is said to be worth $1.5 billion. Ah, the wonders of the Internet!

You do not have to be on the Internet solely to sell or distribute products or services. You can be online to deliver a message like 15-year-old McKay Hatch, founder of The No Cussing Club™ (`nocussing.com`), which was created to bring about awareness to language and how we use it.

McKay Hatch

IN HIS OWN WORDS *When I was in elementary school, I never really heard any of my friends cussing, but it seemed like when I got into middle school, all of my friends started cussing. That really bothered me.*

It took me a couple of weeks to actually get enough courage to tell my friends, "I don't like the words you are using." I finally ended up telling my friends, "If you want to hang around me, I really don't want to hear you cuss." So my friends didn't cuss around me anymore, which I thought was pretty cool.

Later on in the eighth grade, they came back to me and they said, "Hey, McKay, it's because of you that we don't cuss." And I thought that was really cool and that's when I came up with the idea of the No Cussing Club. And I told them the next day about it and they liked it and so we made some flyers and passed them out to about 50 of our friends and we had our first official No Cussing Club meeting on June 1, 2007.

The following year, the club's membership rate increased to 100 members but it really took off with the launch of the website. In only six months, it gained over 10,000 members, including people from all 50 states and many countries around the world. Upon joining, members make a commitment to The No Cussing Challenge, a pledge to improve their lives and the lives of others through better language. Their motto, leave people better than you found them, unites the over 25,000 current members…and it is still growing!

Do you think McKay has a niche market? Of course! And the Internet has been his vehicle to reach it! The website and membership are free, with the exception of t-shirts and wristbands available for

McKay Hatch

purchase, so the monetary value of his venture is still small. But McKay has quite a few plans, including a book that will take him and his organization to the next level. The main reason I had to share his story is because he has stood up for himself, garnered support for his cause and started a movement in his own right.

Now while the Internet has been wildly beneficial since its inception, I believe the future is in the cell phone, the ultimate communication utility device. As reported by the United Nations International Telecommunications Union (ITU), the number of mobile cellular subscribers will reach four billion in 2008. Just like there is a massive contribution from today's youth for iPhone applications, condensed versions of programs that you would run on a regular computer, I forecast that they will continue to design and profit from even newer cell phone applications for years to come.

MY CHALLENGE TO YOU

Who is your target market? Thoughtfully answer this question in your journal or in the space provided. If you were to start today, who would you most like to influence and forever change in a positive and powerful way? Even if you do not know your million-dollar idea, take some time to think about who can benefit the most from what you have to offer.

MY TARGET MARKET:

_____

_____

_____

_____

Grow rich in your niche. You have unlimited options and the world is anxiously awaiting your magnificent ideas!

CHAPTER 6

DREAM TEAMERS

One constant among all of these young entrepreneurs is the tremendous support they receive from their family, friends and community. *Creating change is not something that you can do alone and it is imperative to have a strong network of mentors, advisors and peers.*

Jason O'Neill is a 13-year-old, self-proclaimed business man. He is the creator of Pencil Bugs Plus (pencilbugs.com), whimsical pencil toppers "made by a kid, but not just for kids!" Each Pencil Bug comes with a Certificate of Authenticity that includes its name, the date it was born and care and training instructions. Jason has already expanded his initial product into a broader line of items featuring the eight pencil bug characters, but there were times when he wanted to call it quits.

Jason O'Neill

IN HIS OWN WORDS

I [have always] wanted to make money and [run] businesses. Since I was five I was doing lemonade stands and hot chocolate stands and cookie stands outside of my house.

So I've been wanting to make money and doing business for a very long time.

[Pencil Bugs] started three years ago from a little craft fair that my mom was doing. She said that if I wanted to make money, which I did, that I had to come up with my own idea. I didn't give up and I started trying out some ideas. Since I like school, and I know not all kids do, and you need pencils for school, I wanted to make something to go on top of a pencil and then Pencil Bugs were born.

I've had a lot of support from my parents. They've been what has kept me going. A lot of times I've wanted to quit. That's one of the things that I'm really thankful for, because out of the too many times to count that I've wanted to stop this thing, they kept me going.

When I spoke with Jason I told him I was so proud of him because, although he gives his parents a great deal of well-deserved credit, he is the visionary behind the Pencil Bugs brand. He has already written the first book of a series featuring his characters, has plans for a plush toy for smaller children and a video game as well. He dreams big and hopes to someday create *Pencil Bugs: The Movie.* To have such clearly defined goals and be willing to work hard towards them, especially at such a young age, is pretty remarkable. When I asked him how much his company is worth at this point, he told me he could not tell me because it is a private company. He assured me that as soon as it becomes public, I will be the first to know. He is talking like a seasoned businessman already!

Everyone deserves to be like Jason and have people in their corner, rooting for them and cheering them on in their endeavors. Just think what the Super Bowl would be like without fans. Or the red carpet at the Academy Awards. It is the public display of love and affection that can really make you feel special.

"Wow – Yes, I see – your resume looks good, Dad..."
©Jonny Hawkins

I asked each entrepreneur what they would say to other young people who want to start their own business. Maryanne Barrott said you must have the backing of good people behind you.

IN HER OWN WORDS

MARYANNE BARROTT

My parents have always supported me a hundred percent in whatever I wanted to do. Even if they knew I would hate it, they always let me try the things I wanted to do like take dance lessons or singing lessons, things like that. My parents were always really supportive.

There is so much responsibility in being an adult, even more when you directly impact the lives of children. If you are an adult reading this book and you are privileged enough to be a role model for any young people—whether by family or vocation—I humbly request that you really think through how you are showing up in their lives. McKay Hatch talks about the power of language and I hope that you think carefully about what you say to those who seek your guidance. Be congruent with your intent, thoughts and actions. When someone close to you approaches you with a dream, treat it like the big deal that it is and let them know anything is possible. Be their friend and their mentor.

I have been blessed with 44 mentors and each one shared their wisdom with me in ways I will never forget. My first mentor, who is still a dear friend, was John Reinhardt, my English teacher who turned me on to reading when I was 14 years old. Then when I was in graduate school I discovered the work of Dr. Buckminster Fuller, who I still hail as the smartest guy I have ever known. I traveled around the world with him for seven years and learned to think comprehensively because of him.

The list goes on and each individual mentor gave me distinctions that I consider to be the most valuable gifts I have ever received. From John Reinhardt I got the love of reading. From Bucky I learned comprehensive thinking. And from Chip Collins, my closest mentor and friend, who I still speak to daily, I got the discernment and details of how to speak. Without the influence of these men, I would be a very different person today.

Ephren Taylor, our successful wealth engineer, knows the value

Wolfgang Amadeus Mozart started to compose small and beautiful melodious numbers by age five, and by nine was writing symphonies. Mozart was more than encouraged by his father; he was Mozart's teacher, coach, manager and mentor.

89

of mentors and is honored to be one himself. He said that he always
jokes with kids that the reason he shot for the moon is because all
of his mentors had their own private planes. How can you disagree
with that logic?

Having a mentor means having someone who shows you how they
did it, so you can improve upon that and figure out your own way.
Mentors can even be people you do not know personally. They can be
the athlete of your favorite sports team, the broadcast journalist on
CNN, the Broadway star or even your most beloved author. When
you identify a "dream" mentor, go directly to Google and download
their picture. Print it out and put it beside a picture of yourself so
you can visualize the two of you meeting someday. I assure you that
you will be taking a real picture with them sooner than later.

The amazing thing about mentors is that they can be of any age!
The entrepreneurs highlighted here are already mentors because
they are telling their stories and letting their voices be heard. They
are affecting their peer groups by their example and showing them,
in so many ways, what is possible.

Lately, it is accepted as common knowledge that your peer group
shapes who you become. My mother told me, "Boy, if you hang
around great and inspiring men long enough, you will be a great and
inspiring man." My personal peer group is very limited. They are all
highly productive, very interesting, totally turned on, tapped in and
illuminated. My peer group has a tremendous amount of influence.
I hang with them regularly in person, by computer and telephone
and they are all doing wonders. I am amazed at every level of all the
people I hang out with and that is what I want for you.

Your peer group needs to challenge you, excite you and lift you
up. If it does not do that, you must find a new one! Did you know
you can find a new peer group in books? You can! How about by
listening to audio programs of some of the greatest minds of our
time? You can! Get resourceful. When I was bankrupt and upside-
down 34 years ago, my peer group became self-help action books,
audio programs and biography videos. When I started earning more
money, I could not buy enough tapes and CDs on how to get ahead.
I bought several hundred videos from the Biography Channel on

Andrew Carnegie, Walt Disney, Bill Gates, Mary Kay Cosmetics and Dr. George Washington Carver to name a few. I found the answers I needed at a time when I needed them most. I recommend that you do the same.

MY CHALLENGE TO YOU

Make a list of all the people whom you love, respect and admire. When you have written your list and checked it twice, send each person a note or email of gratitude. Let them know you appreciate what they have done for you. Next, I would like you to brainstorm and soul-storm all of the qualities that you want in your ideal peer group. Just start listing adjectives that speak to you, stimulate you and make you happy.

PEOPLE I LOVE AND ADMIRE:

_____ _____ _____

_____ _____ _____

_____ _____ _____

_____ _____ _____

MY IDEAL PEER GROUP:

_____ _____ _____

_____ _____ _____

_____ _____ _____

_____ _____ _____

SUPERSTAR
at a Glance

AKIANE KRAMIRAK

Age 14
Artist and Poet
Paintings sell for $25,000 to $1 million
<u>artakiane.com</u>

How did you first start your business?

I started painting when I was six, but I started drawing when I was four. It was with pencils or in chalk, but if I didn't have chalk or pencils, I just took food and wrote on the windows or on the table. I just took whatever I could get my hands on.

Around four to seven years old, I started using these pencils and started practicing each day. Then all of a sudden around Christmas time, my mom gave me some pastels and I started pastels and then later acrylics. Someone noticed my talent and I was invited to the *Oprah [Winfrey] Show* and after the Oprah Show, I couldn't believe there were so many people asking for my website. We put up artakiane.com and from there, it was like 10,000 hits a month. It was just amazing, all over the world, people calling me and emailing me and they were so happy that there's something positive on TV now and in the magazines. I'm so blessed and so happy.

Some people wanted to contact me and thank me for what I have done for them, like change their lives in a positive way. They think my paintings are inspirational and hopeful and some of **my paintings inspire kids to keep on doing what they're doing, don't give up and show the love overall for whatever it is they want to do.**

Before I was on the Oprah show, I had no idea who Oprah was and later my mom told me after the show how big she was and how popular she was. To meet Oprah was amazing.

How many paintings have you done, since some take up to three months?

I have completed over 120 works of art.

How do you do these phenomenal spiritual paintings?

I just know that I envision these faces and I met these people through my visions or through real life and I just have this eye that kind of wants everything perfect. If it's not perfect, then I'll make it perfect. I'm a perfectionist in a way. I see the people and I want to paint exactly what I see in my mind and in real life. I don't know how I get these visions or get these images. I just know that I put them on canvas.

Were you trained as a painter?

No, not at all. Actually, I grew up in a family that was not artistic. Somehow one day, I just started drawing these faces and started practicing with myself and one day I just kind of progressed more and more and more. None of them are painters or artists except for my baby brother; he's the abstract artist.

How did you paint the picture *Father Forgive Them?*

I found the model after two years and it came through the front door and it was just a miracle itself. But after I painted that painting after 70 hours, these people from all over the world started calling me saying that is the most precise image that they were seeing in their heads

or in their visions. They said that it was the most realistic painting they've ever seen in the states and it was just overall incredible. I was nine years old at that time and I didn't know how precious these comments were until I got older and it inspired me to do more, to just paint harder. I don't know how I did it. I just do it.

How about the *Prince of Peace?*

I was around eight-and-a-half when I painted that and when I started sketching the model, I don't know what happened. I just switched the position and I absolutely fell in awe and I painted it and actually it was 40 hours and I lost four teeth.

It was really weird, but every day I had new inspiration, new ideas and new details to put in that painting. I was so excited for the next morning to put it on canvas, but it's hard to say. If you see the original painting, no matter where we walk, it always stares at you. It was incredible and yet strange at the same time. It was pretty neat.

Do you sell the original paintings?

We sell the originals, but probably just a few per year. Mostly we do reproductions and prints and most of the people buy those because the originals are usually too expensive for the everyday person.

What is your main passion or purpose with regard to your artwork?

My biggest passion is to share the emotion that I was

painting in the painting, to share that love, to share that connection, so that people can get inspired at the same time and people create their own gift in their heart.

What problems have you had to overcome?

I do not remember all of them. **I just don't remember the problems that came up. I just remember the success that came out of it** and that I'm really, really blessed and happy that it was all meant to be. I'm really happy.

Do you pray, meditate or go inside your mind to do some of these pictures and bring out the luminescence and the radiance?

I believe nature is the key to divinity or to seeing the visions and dreams. Each time when I have that inspiration, I go outside or I just sit on the swing or go to the park or to the beach and that gives me that inspiration, that purity in my mind. And it flows through everything and that has given me so much. I feel so much pure visions and dreams. I really want to commit to almost everybody to go to nature and be like nature. It'll give you so many more ideas and it can purify your heart and your mind. That's what I do almost every day.

[Akiane gets up daily at 4:00am.]

I paint probably for four to five hours. I just paint. I really love it because it's so peaceful and quiet in the morning. Since I have a handful of brothers, when they get up, it's just chaos. It's so peaceful in the morning.

Superstar at a Glance: **AKIANE KRAMIRAK**

Does the talent come to you naturally?

[answered by Akiane's mother, Foreli]

We have a huge 3,000 square-foot gallery right adjacent to the residence that we have been building for the past year and when people come in, they see all these paintings all at once and they see it only as a miracle. Whereas I as the mother who was videotaping her work, who was observing, photographing, recording, just commenting on her work to the public, I see it all as an absolute blood and sweat of Akiane's work and a miracle too. I don't discount that, but where she took off is where her dedication was.

Yes, she did have a wonderful gift and she did have some supernatural experiences when she was younger. As Akiane says, **her gift to God is what she did with that gift that she received, which was her dedication, her passion, her work, her love for what she does, the things that she shares with others** and that's what I see. I see her working no matter what, through thick and thin and there's no such a thing as for her to abandon the work just because she doesn't like something. She can be completely frustrated. Nothing is working and yet she will just continue working and sometimes she has five or six paintings on top of one another. She will not discard that canvas, but she will keep on working on the top, on top, on top, on top up until it works out, but that's what I see. Maybe other people don't see that because they're not here.

Superstar at a Glance: AKIANE KRAMIRAK

What was the supernatural thing that happened to you?

Every day is a miracle, but the most supernatural thing that ever happened to me was probably when I was five and I was actually lifted up into Heaven physically for six hours. My parents, my brothers, the police and everybody was searching for me. My mom considered me kidnapped. She was just terrified. But from my point of view, I was up. I was looking from above. Everything, every move, every step a person took and what I remember, I was split into millions of pieces and I was going through millions of experiences and six hours later, but not in the space time, but in the Earth time, I came back and all I remember is my mom coming and just rushing up to me and crying. She asked me, "Where have you been? We've been looking all over for you." And she was just crying, but I looked up to her and I said, "Mom, I was with God. I have a lot of work to do." And of course at that time, they did not fully understand what I was going through, what I was seeing and who God was, but little by little when they saw me working and trying to do my best with painting and drawing, they kind of grasped that idea that there is something and we have to encourage her.

Ever since then, it has just been miracle after miracle. I'm really blessed to have a family that understands. Unlike other families, they think that their kids or their teenagers are going through a stage and they're just imagining, but I was not imagining for sure. There was no television at our house. We had no papers. No magazines. I believe my mom finally realized there is something and that's kind of how it all progressed and now it's the most fantastic thing that ever happened to me.

Can you explain your painting *The Footsteps of Eternity*?

Well, virtually it's all about the girl that's on the bottom, which represents the earthly self that is going through hard times, struggles and hardships. She has just given up on life, but her heavenly self is pouring some kind of liquid hope, liquid love on her head and I switched their dresses. The earthly self, there's a white background with black spots. The white background represents the purity. The black spots represent the experience we have here on Earth and I switched them. The heavenly self experiences the black in the white spots. The white footsteps are the purity footsteps and that was kind of how I felt when I was traveling, when I was seeing these places and the heavenly self is always with you no matter where I was.

You know it's really different to experience it. It's a lot easier to comprehend, to experience. It's hard to explain, but it's easy to experience it.

Do you contribute?

Oh yes. Actually through my paintings and my poetry, a portion of the purchase of my paintings goes to charities, to churches, to the homeless people and the starving people. It's always a dream, always a goal that I've had since I was really little and I really want to continue with that dream to help people, to help the needy children. And if I don't do that then I feel so empty and if I do help those people, I just feel more comfortable and have to do more and more and it feels so good inside when I do that.

Do you consider yourself an entrepreneur?

I consider myself as part businesswoman, part artist and part sister, a normal kid. I guess I have all three of them.

And you balance them pretty well?

I balance them pretty well and if I don't have at least one of them, I get off balance. My dad started teaching me more about the taxes and the business, the money that's coming in and going out and the art, what it produces. I really loved it. I'm learning things that I need to learn and I'm really happy and excited that probably when I'm 18, the whole business is going to be on my shoulders and I'll be able to do it all by myself with some other help. But it's really interesting to learn and yet to have the painting on the side and just be a normal sister or a normal friend.

Do you have a definition for God?

It's very simple. It is love in unity and I believe that he really wants each one of us to love one another and unify. It's still really hard to give the full meaning of what he wants us to do, but I know he still wants us to love one another.

Are you doing any more spiritual paintings right now?

I'm doing so many different kinds, spiritual, non-spiritual, just everything. The people crave different paintings. It just varies from all different kinds of aspects of views, spiritual, non-spiritual. I'm really happy that

people can relate the differences of the paintings no matter if they're Christians, no matter if they're Buddhists or just anybody. So I have a good feeling that one day I will be able to somehow bring people closer together and closer to God.

How do you define faith?

I believe each one of us has faith, even if you're not rich or not believing. I believe everyone has faith, but I believe that someone needs to tell them that each one of us has a connection to the divinity, has a connection to God. I believe through my paintings, I'll be able to tell people and just raise them up in saying that they have a connection. But some people just don't want to choose that; they don't want to be connected to the divinity. But faith is open and available to each one of us. It's just we need to understand that knowledge and understand where it is going and how it is going. I grab that faith and I grab that hope and I just hold onto it all these years and I never let it go.

But faith, it's complicated to explain. Each one of us has it. We just need to have hope and have faith and have that love inside of us.

You need to have not just the faith or the hope, you need to have that effort, that inspiration, that drive and just keep on moving better, that motivation. Without my mom's motivation or all these comments, I would not be able to be here today because I would not be able to convince myself I could do better, I could do just more precise, more perfect and I'm very thankful for that really.

BUILDING A BRAND TO COMMAND

CHAPTER 7

THE BIZ OF BIZ-NESS

Peer group is by far one of the biggest factors involved with the success of all of the entrepreneurs I spoke with for this project. What so many of them did, and what I am in total awe of, is that they found a way to make their peer group their clients.

They did not go in search of an unknown market; they found what they were looking for in their own backyard. Relationships that they had already established and nurtured, whether in school, at home, in their community or online, became the foundation for their businesses to grow. This is not a factor to be taken lightly. Each of these entrepreneurs discovered their niche in their everyday life, something that has my utmost respect and admiration.

Strong client and customer relationships are crucial in business. Anticipating their needs and giving them what they want, before they even ask for it, is a major component. For Allyson Ames, creating an experience for her customers at Wonderland Bakery has always been a top priority and she keeps that in mind as she contemplates expansion.

IN HER OWN WORDS

ALLYSON AMES

We value our clients, customers and talented staff and everyone participates and enjoys the creative, whimsical environment. I stay focused on keeping the Wonderland experience unique, creating with the finest ingredients and developing the best quality products within a successful and profitable business model, as we scout new locations and explore nationwide expansion opportunities. I am excited about the introduction of our whole new product line—Bake Memories at Home collection of mixes, aprons, tea sets, bake sets; Wonderlicious Storybook; and the animated Allyson Wonderland Storytime Bear by Gund.®

The uniqueness of the Wonderland product and the destination bakery experience will help us grow and prosper in every economic climate. People will always need to celebrate holidays, birthdays, weddings and business occasions. To give or receive a delicious and beautifully packaged gift from Wonderland will always make everyone feel special.

Allyson consistently puts the needs of her clients first and always keeps her hands in the dough, so to speak. Because of all of her efforts and hard work, the valuation of her brand, including intellectual properties, licensing and potential product placement, was at $10 million in 2008. Remarkable!

"Here's your lemonade and here's some descriptive
literature about my franchising opportunities."

©A. Bacall

I cannot say enough how important it is to stay in touch with your market. Martina Butler told me that she is regularly in communication with her audience on emogirltalk.com. They call her audio line and she makes a point of responding to them on her podcasts. Although she is not talking to them live, she feels like she is having a conversation with each of them and really cares about what they have to say. Same thing goes for Ashley Quails on whateverlife.com.

IN HER OWN WORDS

ASHLEY QUAILS

I was getting a lot of questions and I gathered how I actually teach other people. Not only do I offer labs in graphics, I offer the tools to actually learn how to do it yourself, which is why I think the site has been so successful; people aren't left in the dark. They're looking at this and they're saying, "What does this mean?" So I try to teach them exactly what it means and it's just kind of a reference guide as well. We're actually developing website layouts...just for teenagers and young adults, our main target.

It's all done from the users. It's all done from the visitors. They give input and it's important to us as you are our customers. That's what is important in retail. It's important in sales, important in every kind of business; it's just knowing what your visitors, your customers, want.

The level of understanding that each of these young people has about their business is extraordinary. Some of them learned through mentors, some by modeling others and some just by sticking with what felt right. It all comes back to your inner guidance system. It is quietly prompting you and will lead you exactly where you are meant to go. But you do not have to take my word for it.

OLIVIA BENNETT

When I was younger I really relied on my parents for guidance. As I have gotten older I have been much more involved in the business side of my career. I really enjoy both aspects of it. Painting is my love. I get such a rush every time I complete a piece; I really put my heart and soul into each one! The business side has proven to be much more challenging. I try to take something away from every experience, good or bad. I have learned a lot from trial and error. It is not always the easy route, but it has given me experience that I could not have learned from a text book.

I really rely on my intuition. There are many times when I don't know which direction to go. During those times, I really have to trust in God for insight and understanding.

Olivia has the guidance of friends and mentors, but ultimately she trusts herself the most. I have to applaud her because this insight will take her further in business and in life than anything else. And as she said, the business side of business is not always easy, but I know that each one of you is ready and capable to conquer whatever challenges you face. How do I know this? Because you have already shown me! Nathan Nguyen confirmed this belief for me when he told me the following story about his first online order for his retail company.

NATHAN NGUYEN

I lost $4,000 on my first sale because it was a fraudulent order. I did not know any better. I was really excited. We got sales in; I was jumping up and down that people are coming in. I was excited but then I realized it

*was a $4,000 loss. This was the defining point...
stop and quit or stumble forward.*

*I said, "You know what? This is a perfect business
because it will challenge me and force me to
be better." It is all about building who you are
and what you know. Your biggest assets are
information, knowledge and experience.*

*I said, "This will be a wonderful business. If I can
lose $4,000 and figure out how to turn it around,
this will be an awesome venture." Because it is not
the business that is not succeeding, it is the person
who is running the business who is not doing it
correctly. So I had to improve myself...a lot.*

*It took us 18 months before we got out of the red
and I just kept on moving forward. I said, "This
business is a good business. I have to find a way to
make it work." It took us 18 months, but we got out
of the red and it is fantastic. I learned so much and
I made more contacts than I can even believe and
looking back, it is all worth it.*

Nathan, even when confronted with a huge monetary loss, believed in himself and his business. Talk about being a solution! This young man repeatedly amazes me with his work ethic, follow through and complete zest for life.

One point that came up for me when I heard Nathan's story, was that as a business owner or entrepreneur, you can never take your eye off of your company. Whether it is keeping up with your customers, improving your product or reviewing your financials, you have to take ownership of every area. There is no way around it. While there may be areas that you enjoy more than others, each category is of the same level of importance. **You want to have intentional synergy.** What that means is every area of your business is in sync, working together so that all of your efforts combine to give you the best possible results.

MY CHALLENGE TO YOU

Find a comfortable spot where you can let your creative imagination take you two years down the road. What is your big idea? How is it packaged? Who does it serve? Think about how many products you have sold or how many lives you have touched. What does your life look like? Where do you live? Really see your house, your office and the people closest to your heart cheering you on to do more incredible work. Take a few moments to write whatever comes to mind  about your dream life and business. Do it in your journal or in the space provided below.

MY **BIG** IDEA:

_____

_____

_____

_____

_____

_____

_____

The Proverb of Solomon says, "Where there is no vision, the people perish." I want you to be a visionary, but I also want you to create sustainable income that does not own you. The way to do that is to out-think, out-work, out-lead, out-serve, out-deliver and out-perform your competition. You can do it. I am counting on you.

CHAPTER 8

INFINITE TIME

At this point your mind may be whirling
and you may be feeling a bit overwhelmed.
Totally understandable. After each interview
my head was spinning with all of the ideas
and projects of these incredible kids.

There is a heck of a lot to manage in a business and when you are also trying to divide time between school, friends and family, it can become just too much.

Luckily, you have the personal expertise of each of our entrepreneurs to help you as you navigate what to do and where to put your focus first. Because when you are out trying to save the world, as Ephren Taylor told me, you have to pick your battle. He said that over the last five years he has realized the true power of focus. When he first started, he was all over the map, 55 miles an hour. But now his focus has really kicked in, he has matured a tremendous amount and he is able to make wiser business and financial decisions.

Ephren is someone who has demonstrated unyielding discipline. He does not compromise on his goals and will give as much as he can, whenever he can, to make a difference. He has always gone the extra mile and I look up to him for that. When you are dedicated to a mission bigger than yourself, it involves long hours and hard work. This is the part where passion plays a significant role, because when you are doing what you were born to do, the rest does not seem to matter.

Maryanne Barrott said that she has learned the most from experiences that turned out differently than she had hoped or planned.

IN HER OWN WORDS MARYANNE BARROTT
One of the things I've learned, especially when you're starting out, is it's not about how much product you're selling, but about the exposure that you're getting. I did a conference in Boise, Idaho. It was a women's conference and it was two days, pretty much all day long. It was Saturday and Sunday and I didn't sell nearly as much as I had expected. But the exposure that I got to different people and the advice I got from others was really, really important.

As a business owner, you may spend countless hours working, but the pay off—monetary or not—is always worth it.

IN HER OWN WORDS

ALLYSON AMES

I know a lot of people who think it's great to own your own business; however it really means you get to work harder and longer than everybody else and make it appear effortless. Whatever career path you take, make sure you are fully committed to going the distance. Your passion will energize and help you over the rough spots when you need it.

For me, Wonderland is my dream. It has been long hours, seven days a week; however, it never feels like work. I am doing what I love in an amazing

"Benjamin, you have to take a break from creating corporate websites and study for tomorrow's spelling test."

©A. Bacall

Steve Martin, famous comedian and actor, at age 10 was working at Disneyland shelving guide books, where he taught himself magic, juggling, playing the banjo and creating balloon animals. By 15 he was working for Disney as a performer.

environment that makes me feel happy, working apron to apron with my mom and talented staff, touching people's lives in a sweet and powerful way. I am very blessed.

Work hard, play hard, right? ***I believe that ultimate fulfillment is finding a way to blend work and play together.*** I am fortunate to be at a time in my life where I can easily mix the two together when and where I choose. But if you are a teenager or young adult, you must find a way to balance work and play...school work and play, that is. I personally believe a business interest can actually stimulate focus and discipline for better results, and for most students, better grades.

"I've got a meeting with my board of directors...
as soon as I finish my homework."

Jason O'Neill takes great pride in his school record. He has been getting straight A's as long as he can remember and plans to continue that streak. Even though Pencil Bugs is taking up a good portion of his time, he still makes sure to be a kid. He plays video games, watches television and plays with his friends. But he also knows that working hard now will have significant payoffs later.

So do you know how to juggle? It is definitely a skill you learn by doing. Jasmine Lawrence has become the master of it as she enters her senior year in high school.

IN HER OWN WORDS

JASMINE LAWRENCE

Trying to be a CEO of a company, but also still being 17, it's really challenging. I got through my junior year OK and everyone says that's the toughest year and I'm hoping that senior year will be more relaxed just focusing on college applications and things like that. Having to travel to see different places and missing chunks of school at a time is probably going to be difficult for me. I'm in an engineering academy so I'm taking these specialized classes that you can't just make up. Just having the hands-on experience in the classroom is what really gets you the good grades and what really gets you an understanding of the material. School is a huge number-one focus for me but just balancing business and school and family time and friend time and life in general is just really big for me.

I would say [I spend] eight hours a day trying to be an engineer. All the time I spend in school is working to that same goal of computer engineering. When I get home it's really flexible with EDEN. I can work all night and then not work at all the next day just to clear my mind. I never want to overload myself. I'll write a speech for

Walt Disney had very early interests in art and he would often sell drawings to neighbors to make extra money. By age 18 Walt joined the Red Cross and was sent to France, where he drove an ambulance and chauffeured Red Cross officials. His ambulance was covered from stem to stern—not with stock camouflage, but with Disney cartoons!

119

something and then I'll go see a movie or go out to dinner with my family. Mixing everything in there and making sure I'm not too stressed out or too tired or wishing that I never went into this, but just making sure that I keep myself happy and I keep the business running well and I keep my grades up is just a system I have.

Jasmine is right. You have to implement a system that works for you. When all is said and done, your health and your happiness are what matter most above all else.

Nathan Nguyen shared his own system for personal improvement and balance. He said that he makes sure to take time *away* from his business so that he can focus *on* his business and look at it from another perspective. For Nathan, he finds relief in reading. I recently coauthored 101 e-books that are available on youpublish.com. The topics range from *Chronic Profitability* and building your confidence to the spiritual, *Why the Saints are Saintly and the Sages are Sage*. Nathan told me that he has started to read one e-book per day...not once...not twice...but three times! He copies notes onto his blackberry, reflects on them and will add more ideas as they come. Why does he take the time to do this? He said it is because reading is good, but applying and living is much more impactful. For Nathan, any process that will help take him from who he is to who he is meant to be is well worth it.

MY CHALLENGE TO YOU

How much do you value your time? If you had to account for every hour of the day, no exceptions, could you do it? Are you aware of where you put your focus and what takes up most of your attention? Turn the page—for at least three consecutive days, I want you to keep a daily log of every hour. Yes, I mean every hour. From the moment you wake up to right before you turn off the light to go to sleep. At the end of the three days, take out your log and circle every hour that you consider time well spent. See how that stacks up against time wasted. You may be surprised at the results.

Are you making the most of every day? I hope you are and my desire for you is to want as much for yourselves as I want for you. You deserve to have a life rich with prosperity and overflowing with abundance. Sound good?

DAY 1　　　　　**DAY 2**　　　　　**DAY 3**

	DAY 1	DAY 2	DAY 3
4AM			
5AM			
6AM			
7AM			
8AM			
9AM			
10AM			
11AM			
NOON			
1PM			
2PM			
3PM			
4PM			
5PM			
6PM			
7PM			
8PM			
9PM			
10PM			
11PM			
MIDNIGHT			
1AM			
2AM			
3AM			

CHAPTER 9

GIVING TO MAKE A LIVING

How would it feel to wake up every day knowing
you already have everything you need?
And whatever excess there is you would gladly
give it to someone else...just because?
What can you accomplish with this type of mindset?
Who could you reach, help and raise up?

I am excited and delighted because all of the kids you have gotten to know come from this place of abundance. They feel blessed by their good fortune and want to share what they have with others. Their lives are brimming with possibility and there is more than enough to go around. And believe me, they give freely. Each of them had to have some form of tithing involved with their business to be included in this book. That was my most important criteria.

"Now that we're a success, I would like to give back to the community. I'll give the office chair back to Mr. Herbert down the street. I'll give the phone system back to Mrs. Martin on the corner. I'll give the bookshelf back to our neighbors, the Dexters..."

©Jonny Hawkins

Maryanne Barrott told me that her family has always been involved with community service and she grew up in an environment where giving back had huge importance. She loves to share what she has learned, especially to children, so she gives of her time and resources to a local elementary school in her hometown. She has set up presentations, conferences and has rallied the support of local business to fund a scholarship for aspiring entrepreneurs.

Chelsea Eubank uses her company, Faithful Fish, primarily to raise money for charities. She told me the greatest part about her business is not the money but helping people. When asked what is most rewarding, she told me it is writing the checks out to her charities. Proceeds from her company currently go to the Fellowship of Christian Athletes, Feed the Hungry and multiple local charities in her community.

I have always been a proponent of residual income and residual philanthropy. This means you set your business up to have a steady stream of money coming in and you make sure to have a good quantity going back out. How much you contribute is the greatest measure of your success and it is something you can start doing right away. Even if you are unable to make a monetary contribution, you can give of your time, your heart, your mind or your intent.

For Jason O'Neill, tithing has been a part of his business since the very beginning. The day he realized he could make money with his Pencil Bugs, the next big decision was to find a place to donate to children. His one stipulation was that his funds had to go directly towards helping the kids. For the first two years of his business he donated to HUGS Foster Family Agency, a local foster agency in Temecula, California. Recently he started donating to the Rady Children's Hospital in San Diego because there are many kids that need care and support. He personally puts together and hand delivers goodie bags to the children.

When you live in abundance you always have more than enough to share and your resources continue to grow.

Oprah Winfrey, talk show host and philanthropist, gave her first speech recital at age 3 during an Easter Service, becoming known as "the little speaker." Despite a traumatic family life, she pursued public speaking. By age 19 Oprah was offered a job for CBS as a co-anchor—where she pretended to be Barbara Walters.

MY CHALLENGE TO YOU

If you had $1 million to give to each of the charities of your choice, what would they be and why? Take a moment to write down your top charities, then review your list and pick the one that is nearest and dearest to your heart. Fill in the Philanthropic Pledge below and choose a completion date in the not-so-distant future. Copy this pledge and put it somewhere you can see it every day as a reminder of what really matters. You may be surprised at the opportunities that will start to show up.

MY TOP CHARITABLE CAUSES:

_____ _____

_____ _____

_____ _____

∽ MY PHILANTHROPIC PLEDGE ∽

I will contribute $1 million to _____ because

_____

by _____ .

Signature: Date:

_____ _____

Ephren Taylor lives and breathes this philosophy in his socially-conscious investing and development business. He supports churches across the country by helping hardworking members get out of debt and into housing. In turn the church congregation thrives and hope is restored within communities. He told me, "Instead of letting drug houses be across the street, we are going to buy it back, put it back together and let a family who deserves to have a home be inside of that house and take this neighborhood back." Ephren is truly a hero and he has a multitude of faith in his work and his God.

I would be remiss if I did not mention the power of believing in something greater. Regardless of your religious or spiritual beliefs, I bet it is safe to say we all have faith in something. I know that I do. Faith, the Apostle Paul teaches in Hebrews 11:1 is "Substance" (of things hoped for) and "Evidence" (of things not seen). I hope for lots of things not seen. As I hold on to my dream unceasingly and relentlessly, sooner or later it manifests, most times in surprising ways.

"Can you hold on? I'm meeting with the chairman
of the ethics committee."

©Jonny Hawkins

I have faith in the invisible. My world is my imagination turned inside out. I take the invisible in my mind and make it visible. All my books start with a blank page and that page excites me because I know in advance, thanks to my abiding and everlasting faith, that I can fill it and it will be worthwhile, helpful to my readers and life changing.

I dream an idea in my mind and keep sculpting it in my imagination until I realize it. I dreamt that I could be a best-selling author and I held on to my imaginative dream. I interviewed 101 best-selling authors and asked how they wrote and how they marketed their books. They generously shared their experiences. I took notes, wrote out what they did, put my post-it notes on the wall and prioritized them. My dream started to take on a reality of its own.

I know I must *feel* the truth of what I faithfully want before I can have the vibration that will manifest it into my reality. I have deep faith that God-In-Me wants me to create my results. Christ taught, "Greater is he that is in you, than he that is in the world." My spiritual source inside is bigger than my every problem, my largest challenge and my greatest opportunity. I merely need to decide to fully use my faith and not let my little fears cloud my thinking or get in my way. I will rock on to success, achievement and glory.

The Universe aspires to help us in all that we do and I think it is pretty clear that we have big tasks ahead of us. Individually and collectively we make choices that affect our future. There is a great deal of comfort in knowing you are not alone. Olivia Bennett wholeheartedly believes that she is being supported by a higher power.

IN HER OWN WORDS OLIVIA BENNETT

I have always had faith. When I was going through cancer there was so much happening to me that I didn't understand...so many unanswered questions. It was difficult being so young and not understanding why I was in that position. Having said that, I knew in the end I was going to be OK.

GIVING TO MAKE A LIVING

I feel that God has blessed me with his incredible gift and I am responsible to use it every way I can. I know that He is going to work through me to affect the lives of others. I think that I have been faced with certain trials in my life, especially leukemia, so that I can reach out to others that are struggling. I believe that God is in control and that He is directing my path.

A sense of relief washes over you when you give up your hardships and uncertainty to something greater. Chelsea Eubanks said her tragedy brought her closer to her faith and to God. Chauncey Holloman has faith in her abilities and says that her talents are from God. And Nathan Nguyen is thankful to his God and his parents who triumphed over adversity and gave him the life he has now. Nathan's story will touch you at the core of your being and I know he will be publishing his own book very soon. Without giving anything away, one thing he told me still echoes in my mind.

Nathan is originally from Vietnam. His father, a Major in the Vietnam War, was injured, taken prisoner and held captive for over nine years. During that time he prayed for his family and his community. Today Nathan says that everything he does is fulfilling the prayer of his parents. Due to his parent's good will and life of service to others, Nathan feels blessed. His parents were so good to him and all of the gifts that he has are because of them. Nathan is so grateful to God for the opportunities he has and every day is a celebration of his freedom and his future.

Do not wait to give yourself the gift of faith—whatever shape it takes for you. You are entitled to all of life's riches and I assure you they will come ten-fold when you use the resources within you and around you to make a difference.

LIVE BIG

When our journey together first began, I told you there were patterns among all of the kids featured in this book and there were key distinctions that they each employed to get them where they are today. In their own words, each entrepreneur has shared their stories, their highs and lows and their extraordinary achievements. These young people from around the country, who have never met, all followed the same principles to realize their dreams.

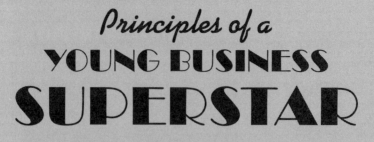

Principles of a
YOUNG BUSINESS
SUPERSTAR

1. Creativity causes your talents to surface.

2. Passion unleashes your potential.

3. Implementation is what takes you from being a dreamer to a business superstar.

4. A problem is just a solution that has not yet been discovered!

5. Grow rich in your niche through total market penetration.

6. Creating change requires a strong network of mentors, advisors and peers.

7. Intentional synergy within your company causes every area of your business to work together to give you the best possible results.

8. Ultimate fulfillment is blending work and play together.

9. When you live in abundance you always have more than enough to share and your resources continue to grow.

The incredible thing about principles is that no matter who you are or where you come from, they still apply to you. They apply to everyone. In my book, *The One Minute Millionaire,* I said:

Principles generate the same result each and every time—no matter where, when or who uses them. Principles work when you work them. Gravity is a principle. When you wake up in the morning, you don't have to question which way your foot will go when you get out of bed. It goes down, never up. Likewise, two times two always equals four. It never equals five. Principles don't wear out, rest out, or give out. They last forever. They are timeless and tireless. Principles cannot be overused. Life is the process of discovering principles—of discovering what works.

The young entrepreneurs have used the principles. They have been the stars of this book. They have shown us what can be done because they are doing it already. As I said in the beginning, they wow my heart, mind and soul with their genius and I am on pins and needles to see what they—and YOU—do next. I can hardly wait! But until then, I will send you off into the world with some final thoughts from Jasmine Lawrence, who has so eloquently articulated the purpose of this book.

IN HER OWN WORDS

JASMINE LAWRENCE

Do something that you love to do that you won't just want to give up one day. It might be easier to take something that pops into your head, but you need to look deep inside yourself; you need to look inside your heart. You need to find not only something that you really like to do, but something that you're good at, something that you have a passion for. That's what my mantra is. Find your passion and live your dream.

You really need to find something that you love to do, something you can do every day. Because when times get hard your passion and your love for what you do is the only thing that's going to keep you going. Even if you're making zero dollars and you don't know where you're going to go next, just having that fire, having that passion, and having that goal to work for is what's really going to matter in the end. Then being happy and being completely satisfied with every single step forward and every step back that you make is really going to make you the person that you are when you get older.

Even if you are an adult, take advantages of your resources. It doesn't matter if you're 55 or 15; I believe that anyone can do whatever they want, especially living in the country that we live in where opportunity is limitless.

With that said, I wish you a life of joyous abundance where you get to make a difference that makes a difference that makes an impactful, permanent and profitable difference!

Until we meet again…

BUSINESS STRATEGIES
FROM ALLYSON AMES

WONDERLAND
BAKERY

BUSINESS STRATEGIES FROM ALLYSON AMES

Create a Plan and Roadmap Develop a Concept and Development Plan, Strategic Plan, Business Plan, Marketing Plan, Business Financial Plan and an Exit Strategy Plan with specific goals before you start your business.

Dream Wonderland Bakery started as a dream; however I broke it down into baby steps:

1. Concept and Development Use your heart and passion.

2. Strategic Plan Where you want to be in 1, 5, 10 years and how you will get there.

3. Business Plan There are many software packages that can help you here.

4. Financial Plan Start with realistic goals, test the market and expand on your success.

5. Marketing Plan Be creative, engage the media and live your brand.

6. Brand Development and Design Design and create the best and finest ingredients and products. Your name is on everything that leaves the store.

7. Continued Development Build your target market and go deep and wide with products that follow your target market. Create alliances and affiliates.

8. Expansion Plan For when the time and opportunities are right (airport, nationwide retailers).

9. Exit Strategy We initially created a five-year plan. I visualized growing a sweet and powerful brand and positioning Wonderland Bakery as an acquisition by a public company to take my dream worldwide.

Review and Update Periodically update progress, milestones and numbers and make any adjustments necessary.

Stay Disciplined Stay open to opportunities, however instead of "No" use "Not yet." Always keep the door open when great opportunities come up and the timing is not right.

Example: The first part of our brand expansion was to create our animated Allyson Wonderland Storytime Bear with Gund.® The bear would become our "Sweet Ambassador" and tell our Wonderland Story to the world. Consistent with the quality of products and ingredients for everything Wonderland, we selected Gund, who is one of America's top 50 brands. Although only a few individually at Gund were part of the Allyson Wonderland Bear project, word of the "special new product" was leaked and we were approached by a prestigious retailer with over 100 stores nationwide to carry our Wonderland brand footprint in each store. Although this was not part of our business plan, we were thrilled about the potential association and confirmation we had a desirable brand and products.

The nationwide retailer wanted every product we produced (30 at our initial launch and now we have over 100). After exploring the opportunity, we determined that it was too soon to commit to this large of a project and deliver everything ordered timely. We were still learning the new design and product development process, so our initial answer was, "Not yet."

We proceeded to test the market launching our entire Wonderland Bakery Collection in a scalable model of our store at one of the most prestigious shopping destinations in America, South Coast Plaza, Costa Mesa, California. Our Wonderland Bakery Collection was a phenomenal success.

This was a valuable lesson learned. Although initially the offer was tough to pass up, you get one chance to get it right with these Herculean opportunities. When the time is right and you have the product, staffing and infrastructure in place, the best opportunities will occur and bring you an exponential result without the headache and heartache.

We now have a choice of several nationwide retailers and expand markets. Additionally, we have negotiated better terms for the continued growth of the brand.

Flexibility for Growth As your business grows, give yourself room for growth; however, your plan should not take an amoeba approach, changing shape with every opportunity.

Example: When we first started Wonderland we were approached by a TV talk show to feature our tasty products on a nationwide show. We would need to hop on a plane for the East Coast with products for the audience within a few hours of the call. Our website was not fully operational with e-commerce fulfillment; we only had three telephone lines and not enough staff to handle volume orders yet. Although we could have gained notoriety overnight, frustrated calls and consumers can have a negative impact. It may have been for all the wrong reason, so we answered, "Not yet."

When the next opportunity came knocking, ABC's The View Whoopi Goldberg designated our Gingerbread Man Cookie, "The Best in the Country." Within one hour of the broadcast, we received 700 internet orders and the phones have not stopped ringing. This time we were ready, we had built a strong organization, e-commerce website, infrastructure, staff, and we were able to capture the opportunity, which equated to revenue and new customers nationwide.

The timing of opportunities is crucial. Initially it was difficult to say "not yet;" however, it was the best decision for us. Now we have a proven brand, product line and more nationwide expansion opportunities. It is our goal to have every new customer who is introduced to our brand become a lifelong customer. One day, I hope Wonderland will be a public company or part of an international brand. (Emeril was purchased by Martha Stewart's Omni Media for $1 billion; Howard Schultz, founder of Starbucks, helped to expand the Pinkberry concept with capital and management.)

Philanthropy Identify a percentage of your business revenue or "in kind" donations to benefit the community and what speaks to your heart. Your generosity will come back exponentially.

Example: When we created the business plan a percentage of all revenue was set aside for our foundation, Thanks a Million Cookies and Cupcakes. We contribute to many organizations that impact community, quality of life, education, animals and our planet. There were some weeks when we first started in business that we made more contributions than sales, however this generosity has brought us great blessings of abundance.

Network Join business and professional associations and associate with like-minded individuals and business owners. This helps create a buzz and will generate reciprocal business from within the organizations.

Advisory Directors Create a strong and diverse Advisory Board of Directors and Board of Directors. It will help you stay focused, keep you accountable to your strategic plan and core business and be a great sounding board when making tough decisions.

Example: When we were ready to expand and appoint a Board of Directors and Management, this was a great place to start, as these influential individuals have helped to incubate the company and they understand the objectives and culture of the company.

Passion Fall in love with your business and keep the passion. This will carry you when you need more energy and hours in the day.

Example: I am always excited to share my story and it is an honor and privilege to be an inspiration for other young entrepreneurs or Mothers and Daughters to create and follow their love, passion and dreams.

Values Create a mission statement about your business, culture and translate that message in all that you do.

Example: Some of the best memories I have are baking with my mom. I wanted to share that experience with others and developed the "Bake Memories at Home" Collection of dessert mixes. With a focus on family, baking at home offers a unique experience that transcends generations and cultures. Whether a child is young enough to be content licking batter from a spoon or old enough to measure ingredients, baking is not only a great way to bond with children, it's also a way to develop math and verbal skills, improve confidence, create memorable family traditions and encourage creativity.

Customers Create an experience so unique for your customer and you will build a loyal following.

Example: Our customers can grow up and old with our edible and non edible products. When we are introduced to a customer or family, our goal is to help make everyone they know and love feel special with something from Wonderland. Every season, holiday or occasion is a reason to celebrate "Wonderliciously."

Partners and Employees Treat your partners and employees with the utmost respect. This translates to customer service and the entire culture of your company. Offer the best benefits to your employees; they are your family.

Management Build the infrastructure for growth. Appoint key people to be part of your dream and when you expand, you have a strong foundation. Advisory Directors are a great resource when the time comes to expand these positions.

Timeless Concept, Brand and Product Wonderland Bakery has a product mix that appeals to a multi-generation customer profile. The concept is timeless, is not a fad and has long legs with branding that can touch a wide range of products for decades.

Product Diversity Expand your core business products or services. We developed a Sweet Guerilla Marketing campaign for business clients. The business client's success became our success with expanded orders.

Example: Developing business and corporate clients are an important part of our growth. We provide scalable unique branding for business customers from small to Fortune 100 companies. The National Business of Women Business Owners selected Wonderland Bakery products as their logo cookies. They used our brand on their National Corporate Gift Award. They offer it to 9,000 members nationwide. This endorsement translated into nationwide exposure and revenue.

Website Create a unique and dynamic website that will showcase your product and translate to sales. When you select a website developer, look for a long-term relationship and get references. Build a strong online customer network and use social networking sites, including YouTube, Facebook, Twitter and Flickr.

Example: To expand the Wonderland Bakery experience from brick-and-mortar stores to the website was a challenge. After months of working with a web developer, we were ready to launch the website and the company went out of business. This was a blessing in disguise as we ended up with a better website in the long run; however, the delay was costly in terms of time, opportunities and revenue. We now ship nationwide with a website that captures the essence of Wonderland Bakery and even the cursor sparkles!

Marketing & PR We have found the best media and exposure for Wonderland has been living the brand. Get ready to tell your story and create a media kit with the background, fact sheet, biography and story of your company. This is a necessary tool when you approach the media or they call you. When you tell your business story, have fun, get creative and share your passion

Example: We created a beautiful cookie as a favor for a high-profile charitable event. The cookie was sent to the media (our name was on the packaging) with the information on the event. One of the business reporters ended up writing a great feature story on our business that also included our philanthropic contributions after the event.

Don't Expand Too Quickly Get your business on solid footing before you expand your brand. Replicate systems and the experience of your brand to keep a consistency and efficiency in your business.

Have Fun I work apron to apron with my mother and we have given birth to Wonderland together. That is the most amazing part of this business venture. Our strengths complement each other, we have a young, energetic and talented staff that has been here from the day we opened our doors and continues to expand. We love what we do and touch people's lives in a creatively, delicious way. Now with our third anniversary product brand launch, our new Ambassador—Allyson Wonderland Storytime Bear™ by Gund, our "Bake Memories at Home" collection of desserts and our lineup of tasty and branded products, we will take our Wonderland Bakery experience to the world!

RESOURCES TO RICHES

Mark Victor Hansen

Mark Victor Hansen
markvictorhansen.com

Mark Victor Hansen Foundation
markvictorhansenfoundation.org

Mark Victor Hansen Recommends
mvhrecommends.com

Hansen House Publishing
hansenhousepublishing.com

Our Young Entrepreneurs

Allyson Ames
wonderlandbakery.com

Maryanne Barrott
maryannesown.com

Olivia Bennett
oliviabennett.com

Martina Butler
emogirltalk.com

Chelsea Eubank
faithfulfish.com

McKay Hatch
nocussing.com

Cameron Johnson
cameronjohnson.com

Chauncey Holloman
officialharlemlyrics.com

Akiane Kramarik
artakiane.com

Jasmine Lawrence
edenbodyworks.com

Nathan Nguyen
instrumentalsavings.com

Jason O'Neill
pencilbugs.com

Ashley Quails
whateverlife.com

Ephren Taylor
themillionairelifestyle.com

Networking and Connecting with Other Young Entrepreneurs

CEOExpress
ceoexpress.com/default.asp

Facebook
facebook.com

LinkedIn
linkedin.com

MySpace
myspace.com

The Collegiate Entrepreneurs' Organization
c-e-o.org

The Young Entrepreneurs' Alliance
nyea.org

Twitter
twitter.com

YoungBiz
youngbiz.com

Young Entrepreneur
youngentrepreneur.com

YouTube
youtube.com

Youth Action Net
youthactionnet.org

Small Business Funding

Business Finance
businessfinance.com

Small Business Administration
sba.gov

Funding Universe
fundinguniverse.com

Magazines

Black Enterprise
blackenterprise.com

Business Week
businessweek.com

Entrepreneur Magazine
entrepreneur.com

Forbes Magazine
forbes.com

Inc.
inc.com

Smart Magazine
smartmagazine.com

Success Magazine
successmagazine.com

The Economist
economist.com

Wired
wired.com

Young Money
youngmoney.com

Business Applications

Article Submission Service
submityourarticle.com

Google Adsense
adsense.google.com

Google Calendar
google.com/calendar

MediaFire
mediafire.com

MySpace Pay Per Click
advertise.myspace.com

Yahoo Pay Per Click
searchmarketing.yahoo.com

YouPublish
yousendit.com

YouSendIt
youpublish.com

Technology

Adobe
adobe.com

Apple
apple.com

CNET
cnet.com

iLounge
ilounge.com

Technology (cont.)

MakeUseOf
makeuseof.com

Microsoft
microsoft.com

Phone Scoop
phonescoop.com

TechCrunch
techcrunch.com

At the time of the printing of this book all websites referenced have been verified.

ACKNOWLEDGMENTS

The Richest Kids in America came into being because I saw that we are in the most challenging economic time ever.

I think this book can help turn our economy back on and get it rocking.

I met most of these kids and they impressed my soul. I am a visionary leader and could easily see how their inspiring stories could lead us out of the problem and into profitability and productivity. These young people are building businesses and empires. I believe their stories will impress and inspire every reader to quit thinking what cannot happen and get into thinking there is a future, hope and new possibilities.

My dream is to take these young superstar entrepreneurs on the seminar trail and onto TV to share their brilliance, wisdom, inspiration, dreams, hopes, prayers and experiences with audiences. I have had them talk at my Mega Seminars and all attendees get uplifted, enchanted and enlightened to the *feeling* that they can do it.

I want to acknowledge the people that helped make this process start and then happen.

Liora Mendeloff was there at the beginning of this process when it went from curious idea to creativity to a real book. I thank her for letting me reiterate my dream incessantly. Continually she offered brilliant advice, wisdom, patience, kindness and encouragement.

Stephanie DeMizio was my creative content development producer. She worked tirelessly to make a superb product that inspired even her.

Chaz DeSimone, my graphic designer, is a true perfectionist. His passion for this project came through in his design and the finished product has exceeded all of our expectations.

Patti Coffey, my chief operating officer, kept my companies and enterprises effectively purring while I poured my soul, mind and brain into the book.

Debbie Lefever, my executive assistant, used to work as a doctor dealing with head and neck injuries and says that, relatively speaking, my problems are easy to solve, do not drive her crazy and have lots of positive benefits. She keeps my time free enough to work on multiple projects simultaneously and still get them all done.

I thank the parents of all the kids who saw the end from the beginning and kindly let me interview their children.

I appreciate all the many who said, "Do it," and those I have inadvertently forgotten to thank, kindly forgive me.

The cartoonists sent us lots of brilliance to choose from and we chose the ones that ideally fit this book to lighten up the deep subject of earning money.

Justin Sachs orchestrated and organized the interviews with delight and excitement and since he is only 19 years old and still in college, he related to all of the kids perfectly.

I lovingly thank Reid Tracy for seeing the vision of this project from its inception and wanting to distribute this book worldwide through Hay House.

ABOUT THE AUTHOR

Debbie Lefever

MarkVictorHansen.com

Focused solely on helping people from all walks of life reshape their vision of what is possible, no one is better respected in the area of human potential than Mark Victor Hansen.

Established as a cultural icon in 1990, Mark and his business partner Jack Canfield created what *Time* magazine called "the publishing phenomenon of the decade," with over 144 million *Chicken Soup for the Soul* books sold worldwide—one of the most successful publishing franchises of all time.

Internationally Known Keynote Speaker and Personality

With his one-of-a-kind technique and masterful authority of his work, time and again he receives high accolades from his audiences as one of the most dynamic and compelling speakers of our time. Having spoken in more than 78 countries, Mark has shared his message of opportunity and action and created powerful transformation in thousands of organizations and millions of individuals worldwide for over 30 years.

Best Sellers

While the Chicken Soup series has achieved phenomenal success, Mark's other bestselling books include *The One Minute Millionaire, Cracking the Millionaire Code, How to Make the Rest of Your Life the Best of Your Life, The Aladdin Factor, Dare to Win* and *The Power of Focus*. Mark has also developed an extensive library of audio and video programs in the areas of big thinking, sales achievement, publishing success and personal and professional development.

Media

His endearing and charismatic style captures audiences' hearts as well as their attention in person, on television or radio and in print.

Appearances: *Oprah*, CNN, the *Today* show, and countless television, print and radio interviews.

Quoted in *Time, U.S. News & World Report, USA Today, New York Times* and *Entrepreneur.*

Entrepreneur

He has targeted the realms of television and feature film for his next steps in his own journey.

Coaching and teaching aspiring authors, speakers and experts on building lucrative publishing and speaking careers through his MEGA seminar series, Mark produces top-notch, results-oriented annual conferences.

Recipient of numerous awards honoring his entrepreneurial spirit, philanthropic heart and business acumen, Mark was inducted into

ABOUT THE AUTHOR

the Sales & Marketing Executive International Hall of Fame and accepted the Horatio Alger Award for extraordinary life achievement in the area of free enterprise leadership.

In conjunction with Mark's Literacy to End Poverty campaign is his online venture consisting of 101 compact e-books filled with life-changing ideas and content. Together with his two partners, he co-authored 101 books in 97 days with the vision of making available an affordable and on-demand library for everyone. They also founded an on-line publishing company allowing anyone to publish and sell their creations on-line: YouPublish.com.

Philanthropist & Humanitarian

Known as a passionate philanthropist and humanitarian, Mark has launched the Mark Victor Hansen Foundation with a mission of promoting entrepreneurial literacy as a means to ending world poverty. The Foundation will create a lasting and impactful difference by creating opportunities for citizens throughout the world in three priority areas: education, economic literacy and entrepreneurial development.